SECRETS TO

10XING

YOUR

BUSINESS

AND CASHING OUT

TAX-FREE

MARC ADAMS

Secrets To 10Xing Your Business

And Cashing Out Tax-Free

by

Marc Adams

Dear Esteemed Reader,

Thank you immensely for choosing this book to join your collection. I Imagine that you've already embarked on an exploration of ideas within these pages, and we couldn't be happier about it!

For nearly 4 decades I've been helping companies scale up, in EMEA, ASIA and North America, doing turnarounds growing the performance, increasing the value, streamlining operations and acquiring as well as exiting businesses but it wasn't until I got diagnosed with stage 4 cancer (which I'm delighted to say I've been lucky enough to beat, more on that in another book maybe) in 2020 that I started to think about documenting the things that you can do to 10x the value of the business and exit tax-free if you're a business owner or even equity stakeholder in a business.

This book, while not covering everything, is intended to bring together a few things that most businesses could implement that would cost-effectively grow the value of the business by either increasing turnover and profit or reducing cost and therefore improving profit as well as oters ways to grow value with mergers and acquisitions (where you could double the business in an afternoon) and how as a business owner you could then exit that business and pay no tax all completely above board and legal. I don't cover everything, it's not the intent to give you War & Peace but I wanted to provide a quick read, packed with practical, implementable secrets that a lot of businesses overlook, that would get most businesses started and the intent is that probably three or four things would be enough to get you there.

There are some other compelling drivers for the book, one is that 9 out of 10 businesses that come to market for sale in the SME sector often end up not selling and the purpose of this book is to provide some secrets, hacks and tricks to improve the value of those businesses so they would be possible to sell for the asking price that owners want. The other driver is more personal in that I want it to support my budding entrepreneurial kids all of whom want to run their own businesses but are not sure where to start, that's a shout-out to my currently 12-year-old Thomas 17-year-old Matthew and 21-year-old Joshua and I'm honoured in privileged that they ask me questions about this and the different kinds of things that they can do. So my hope is that the book, along with my YouTube and other social channels I'm posting to, will provide secrets and guidance for them in the years to come so that they can, in the words of my youngest son Thomas, achieve financial freedom by the time he's 30. Actually, they weren't exact words; what he said was. "Dad, I'd like to get to where you are now, but I don't want to wait until I'm old to do it; how can I do it by the time I'm 30?". Bless him, so my sincere hope is that if I can help any of you and that just a few secrets in this book motivate you and help you to 10x the value of your business then hopefully those same secrets will help my kids when the time is right.

Thank you in advance for picking this book to help you on your journey, I'd love to hear your thoughts along the way.

Regards,

Marc

Contents

Appendix A: Resources for 10X Growth and Tax-Free Exits

Appendix B: Checklists and Templates for Implementation

Introduction: Laying the Groundwork for a 10X Exit

Let's ignite a spark that will transform your business into a roaring blaze of success. You've laid the bricks, you've sweated through the challenges, and now you're eyeing the horizon that spells out "exit." But not just any exit, a grand one where the value of your efforts crescendos to an incredible 10 times its current worth. Imagine setting the stage for a chapter in your business tale that is nothing short of awe-inspiring.

Just pause for a moment and envision the fruits of your life's work multiplied tenfold - a towering testament to the vision and perseverance that have been your companions on this entrepreneurial journey. The path to this pinnacle isn't laden with mere aspirations; it's carved with strategic, methodical actions, and it kicks off with laying a robust groundwork for what we'll call a 10X exit.

Starting with the groundwork means looking at your business not just as your creation but as a machine with innumerable cogs and wheels - each playing an essential role in increasing its operational efficiency, scaling throughput, and ultimately boosting its valuation for that dream exit of yours.

Building such a machine requires a fine blend of optimism and realism. It's about dreaming big but also staring down the cold hard numbers that back your business's value. It's about being honest with what you have, what you want, and how you'll bridge that gap.

Consider this introduction your map to the goldmine. We're not digging for gold that might be there; we're strategizing on how to multiply the reserve you already know exists. You've got your life's effort solidly backing you; your business isn't starting from scratch. It's ripe and ready to grow - you just need to nurture it properly.

How do we start? With vision, but one that is sharply focused on a 10X future. It's like taking your daydreams and drafting them into blueprints—plans that you can act on, measure, and refine. As you think ten steps ahead, we'll delve deeper into what that means, including figuring out your exit goals to keep your eyes on the prize, and taking stock of what you've built to this point.

Then there's the irresistible force of digital marketing. Could there be a more potent tool in the modern business landscape? It's the engine that drives visibility multiplied by infinity, carving out market share with the elegance and precision of a maestro's baton. Harnessing this power effectively could very well be the amplifier to crank your business's value up to eleven.

In parallel, social media mastery can be the siren call that brings the customers to your shores in droves. Channeling the behemoths of YouTube, Facebook, Instagram, and the dynamo that is TikTok, you're looking at creating a brand presence that's not just known but sought out and revered.

Not to forget, growth can sometimes leap rather than step. Picture doubling your business size before your next cup of coffee goes cold - acquisitions done right can be just that impactful. It's not just about adding to your empire; it's about integrating new assets seamlessly to create a whole greater than the sum of its parts.

And we can't forget the allure of high-impact face-to-face sales. Despite the digital wave, nothing beats the trust and rapport established through personal connections. It's about translating handshakes into signed deals and seeing the revenue climb.

Pivoting then to operations - this is where you look inward, fine-tuning every piece of the machine, ensuring that every action, every effort, is streamlined for maximum efficiency. It's where operational excellence meets cost efficiency, laying down the tracks for that 10X trajectory.

Of course, at the heart of this finely tuned machine are systems and processes – the very backbone of scaling with intent. Moving from the 'what' to the 'how', we'll dissect how systemizing is non-negotiable and the very essence of a scalable business.

A stellar business also needs its leaders - a management team that is nothing short of all-star. Identifying these key players, those who will grow your vision as if it were their own, that's a chapter on its own. But suffice to say, empowering your team is empowering your business.

Culture, the ephemeral yet potent energy that drives your team's everyday mood and ambition, will also be pivotal. Think of a positive company culture as an investment that reaps compounding interest in productivity, loyalty, and innovation. It's creating an environment where everyone's striving for that 10X dream – not because they have to, but because they want to.

Moreover, there's magic in delegation and finding the right partners to outsource to - optimizing your labor costs without compromising on quality. In the grand tapestry of your business, every thread counts, and we'll explore how to choose the ones that both strengthen and embellish.

Preparation for your 10X exit culminates in strategizing a tax-free sale – it's your hard-won victory lap, and you deserve every cent of it. Structuring, planning, and laying the legal and financial foundations will ensure that your exit is not just successful, but also maximizes your take-home.

There's a life after the exit—a new beginning, brimming with promise and potential. Picture investing that windfall, projecting your success forward in ways that secure not just your future but that of generations to follow. We'll touch upon that, ever so briefly, because it's the new chapter that awaits after your grand exit.

So, let's start this journey with an unshakeable belief—a resolve to see your business transform, scale, and take off. We're crafting a narrative that culminates in a dazzling 10X exit, with you at the helm, steering your ship confidently into the golden sunset. It's time to lay down the groundwork, and what a formidable edifice it will be.

Chapter 1: Visioning a 10X Future

Imagine walking into your future, where the value of your business isn't just multiplied, but magnified tenfold—this isn't just a dream; it's the canvas for your reality. As we step into a world brimming with untapped potential, I invite you to lean into a bold mindset, one where you're not just running a business, but commanding a force that thrives relentlessly. You're not alone in thinking that a 10X leap sounds like a stretch, but here's the hard-hitting truth—mediocrity can never be your comfort zone. Hold tight to your entrepreneurial spirit and let's carve out a vision so vivid, your business's value doesn't just tick up; it rockets. As we chart this journey, get ready to challenge every assumption you've held about growth and exit strategies. We're placing a lens on not only where you stand now, but also on the pinnacle you're destined to reach. Think of this chapter as the cornerstone of a skyscraper we're constructing together; your ambitions are the blueprint, and 10X growth is the edifice we'll achieve. To the seasoned business owner, it's time to shift gears and throttle forward; your legacy and your wealth are poised to soar like never before.

Understanding Your Exit Goals As we venture further down the path to scaling your enterprise tenfold, let's park for a moment at a pivotal juncture: your exit goals. Knowing where you're headed not only provides clarity but it also fuels your motivation, kindling the fire to push beyond boundaries. Let's go deep into what your finish line looks like— the exit. The conception of your exit isn't merely about selling; it's a complex crescendo of personal aspirations, financial objectives, and the legacy you yearn to leave.

Picture the day you hand over the keys to your kingdom. What does that paramount moment spark in you? Is it a sense of freedom, a wave of relief, perhaps a tinge of nostalgia? It's crucial to sit with these feelings, to understand them, because they're the very essence that will drive your decisions as you build towards this milestone. Your exit goals are multifaceted, blending emotional desires with concrete financial targets. Balance is key, and to strike it, you need to delve into the heart of what you truly want.

Begin by asking yourself, what's the number?—The golden figure that will grace your bank account, granting you the comfort or the adventurous life post-exit you've always imagined. This isn't just any number. It's a number that should make your heart skip a beat, compelling enough to fuel years of dedication. Yet, it should be grounded in reality, informed by prudent calculations and market norms. To arrive there, it'll take more than a stick in the sand; it requires an informed valuation of your business' worth, which we'll cover in detail in the next chapter.

The timing of your exit isn't something you leave to chance. It's a strategic choice, interwoven with market conditions, the state of your business, and personal readiness. The perfect storm of factors that say "now" isn't just serendipity; it's engineered. Think of it like finding the sweet spot in your golf swing—it takes practice, timing, and the right conditions, but once you hit it, the ball soars effortlessly.

Legacy—what's the mark you want to leave on the world, the enduring imprint of your years of labor? Your business might be your opus, something you wish to see continue, to grow, and thrive beyond your tenure. Whether it becomes a family heirloom passed down through generations or a flagship within an industry giant, your legacy plays a crucial part in shaping your exit strategy.

Now, let's talk control. Even as you eye the exit, you're steering the ship, and how you transition away from the helm is critical. Consider this: do you imagine a gradual stepping back, coaching the new leadership into the culture and ethos you've fostered? Or do you prefer a clean break, walking away to explore new horizons the moment the ink dries? Your level of continued involvement post-exit is a linchpin in this equation.

As you articulate your exit goals, remember, the health of your business at sale time isn't a matter of chance; it's a direct outcome of the decisions you make today. A business primed for sale is attractive—profitable, efficient, with a robust management team and a vibrant culture. Every move you make now either adds to its luster or detracts, and understanding this empowers you to sculpt your business into the masterpiece it deserves to be.

Consider the buyer's lens for a moment—what would make your business irresistible to them? Strategic positioning in the market, a unique value proposition, perhaps an unbeatable customer base or cutting-edge technology? Identifying what sets your business apart and doubling down on it will not only 10x your operation but also make it the crown jewel when you're ready to sell. Remember, differentiation is the magnet that attracts premium offers.

Financial freedom post-exit—it's the dream, right? But it doesn't have to be just a dream. With meticulous planning and smart strategies, you can structure your exit so that taxes don't take a bite out of your well-deserved proceeds. Getting savvy with the tax code now will ensure that your financial freedom is as full-bodied as you envision it.

Speaking of financial planning, have you thought about the afterglow of the sale? How you invest and manage that sum will determine the lifestyle you live and the security you feel. Whether it's philanthropy, angel investing, or savoring the good life, your post-exit financial strategy is as important as the exit itself. We'll dive deep into this in Chapter 12—life's not just about reaching the peak, but also enjoying the view from the top.

As you solidify your exit goals, weave them closely with the vibrant fabric of your life. These goals can't stand in isolation—they must resonate with the rhythm of your personal aspirations. Align your business cape with the direction of your life's winds. Only then can you sail smoothly to the destination of your choice. It's more than exit planning; it's life planning with an entrepreneurial twist.

Emotional intelligence plays a role in your exit strategy, too. Exiting can be as emotional as it is financial; there's a piece of you in the business. Preparing for the separation will brace you for the shift, mentally and emotionally. The better you handle this transition, the smoother the changeover will be, for both you and the business you've nurtured.

Changes in technology and market dynamics could also play a decisive role in your exit timing. Stay abreast of trends, innovations, and shifts that could signal the prime time to make your move. Being forward-thinking not only multiplies your business value but positions you strategically in the sale process. We must be as dynamic as the markets we operate in, always ready to seize opportunity.

Consider this journey of achieving a 10x exit as crafting a fine piece of art. Your business is your canvas, your exit goals are the outlines, and every strategy you employ fills in the color and texture. Success is not in speeding through the process, but rather in the thoughtful strokes applied with intention and precision. Understand the essence of your exit, and you'll have the roadmap to a masterpiece that reflects your life's work, culminating in a tax-free, bountiful sale.

Concluding this exploration, remember that your exit goals are not just an endpoint; they're a beacon guiding your every decision. They infuse purpose into your daily grind, allure into your long-term strategy, and ultimately, they're the compass that navigates your business towards a resounding, fulfilling finale. Finetune these goals, breathe life into them, and let them illuminate the path as you journey toward that horizon, where a 10x exit awaits.

Measuring Your Business's Current Value

Measuring Your Business's Current Value is a deciding step that paints a clear picture of where you are on your journey to a 10X exit. It's not just about numbers, it's about understanding the true fabric of your enterprise. Think of it as laying out all the pieces of a complex puzzle on the table. You need to know what you're working with to approach your growth strategically and maximally enhance your business's worth.

Let's get real—measuring the value of your business isn't just about tallying assets and profits. It's a reflection of your sweat equity, your late nights, the risks you took, and the culture you've nursed. It's essential to capture not only the tangible but also the intangible elements that collectively compose the true worth of your life's work.

Start with the Basics—the Numbers. The balance sheet is a snapshot of your company's financial health. But don't let that be the only lens through which you view your creation. Cash flow statements, profit and loss accounts—are these figures telling the story you aimed for when you first started out? Furthermore, consider how these figures translate into a value based on multiples in your industry. Every industry has its benchmarks, and knowing where you stand in relation to these can be eye-opening.

Now, let's talk about profits. They're great, but value is more about sustainability and growth potential. Is your profit trending upwards? Are your revenue streams diversified? Is there potential for more? Your earnings before interest, taxes, depreciation, and amortization (EBITDA), for instance, can be a crucial sign of financial health and attractive for potential buyers.

Assess Your Assets. From real estate to intellectual property, decipher what key assets you own. Tangible assets are often straightforward. It's the intangibles—brand reputation, customer loyalty, proprietary technology

—that are harder to quantify but can make all the difference when measuring your business's value. They are often the deal-makers for an acquirer willing to pay a premium.

Now, picture your market position. Are you a big fish in a small pond, or an emerging player in a vast ocean? Your standing in the marketplace can drastically affect your valuation. Being a market leader or having a strong niche can mean a higher multiple.

Don't overlook your customer base. A loyal and engaged customer base isn't just good for repeat business; it's a gold mine when you're selling your business. Customer acquisition costs can be high, so a stable, satisfied customer base is often a key driver of value.

Examine Your Business Operations. They are the engine of your enterprise. Are they running smoothly and efficiently? Can they withstand your 10X growth plan? Automation, streamlined processes, and a solid management team are signs of an operationally mature business that's ripe for scaling—or selling.

Consider Your Growth Trajectory. Where is your business heading, and at what speed? Growth potential is a massive factor in value. But remember, responsible and sustainable growth often trumps fast, potentially unstable expansion in the long run.

Scrutinize Your Risks. Every business carries risks, and understanding these is pivotal. Legal liabilities, market volatility, and operational weaknesses can all impact your valuation. Addressing these before a sale can not only increase your business's worth but also prevent potential deal-breakers later on.

Finally, imagine walking away from your business tomorrow. How self-sufficient is it? If the success of the business is heavily dependent on you, it's time to start cultivating a business that can thrive on its own. Autonomy adds significant value because it signals to buyers that the business won't collapse when you leave.

Remember, valuing your business is as much an art as it is a science. It requires a keen understanding of not just the financials but also the unique drivers that make your business soar. This value is not fixed; it's something you can build upon with strategic moves and focused intention.

Once you have nailed down your current value, you'll start to see the gaps and opportunities. You'll turn a magnifying glass on areas that can drastically shift your valuation needle north—and that's where the real fun begins. This is your springboard for exponential growth.

As we advance, it's vital to stay grounded in this current value, not as a static figure, but as a launchpad. Your business is a dynamic entity, evolving with every strategic play you make. Continue iterating, optimizing, and strengthing your business; this is a fundamental step toward that monumental 10X exit you're aiming for.

To quote an old wisdom, you can't improve what you don't measure. So take this crucial step seriously. This is more than preparation. It's the foundation upon which your dreams will become reality, your efforts acknowledged, and your legacy cemented.

Embrace this phase of your journey with passion and precision. Knowing where you stand today is the only way to accurately plan for where you want to be tomorrow. And that, my fellow entrepreneur, is how you set the stage for a tax-free sale that truly rewards the empire you've built.

Chapter 2: The Power of Digital Marketing

If you thought digital marketing was just for tech-savvy millennials, think again. In this goldmine of a chapter, we'll dive into how transforming your digital strategy can launch your business valuation into the stratosphere. Imagine wielding the power of Facebook and Google not just to engage with customers, but to systematically convert clicks into hefty sales, because that's exactly what a shrewd digital marketing campaign can do. It's a dynamic field where precision targeting meets creative campaigns, connecting you with buyers who're ready to invest in what you're selling. This isn't your grandson's social media playground; it's a potent tool built on algorithms and analytics that can ratchet your revenue up in ways traditional advertising never could. You'll learn to craft a digital presence that does more than just look pretty—it sells, it engages and it grows your bottom line. By the time you turn the final page, you'll be poised to capture leads, convert sales, and multiply those profit margins, setting the stage for an exit that's as lucrative as it is satisfying. Let's turn the online marketplace into your personal business amplifier.

Maximizing Return on Facebook Ads

Tapping into the vast world of Facebook advertising can be like finding a hidden vault of opportunity—it's ripe for the taking if you know how to crack the code. The key here is not just running ads, but sculpting them into a high-yielding tool that can propel your business towards that illustrious 10X milestone.

The first pillar of a potent Facebook Ads strategy is clarity on your target audience. If you're picturing a scattergun approach, let's redirect that thought. Tailoring your ads to resonate with a well-defined group of Facebook users not only reduces waste but also amplifies the impact of your message. Imagine hosting a dinner party and knowing exactly what tantalizes each guest's taste buds—you'd be the talk of the town. The same goes for crafting ads that speak directly to the desires and needs of your audience.

Now, crafting the ad itself is an art. The visual appeal, the language, and even the call to action need to harmonize. Here's a truth as old as time: an ad that captures attention but fails to motivate action is as good as a car without an engine. Design your ads to not only turn heads but also intrigue minds to the point where clicking through is simply irresistible.

Split testing is your unsung hero in the quest for maximizing your return. Every variable, be it an image, headline, or a color scheme, is up for examination. Run concurrent campaigns with subtle changes to discover what alchemy of elements fuels the most engagement. Like a master chef tweaks a recipe to perfection, you should refine your ads based on performance data. This is operational excellence that your competitors may likely overlook.

While we're navigating through the art of Facebook adverts, let's not forget the importance of timing and relevancy. Leverage the power of seasonality, current events, and trends to make your ads echo with immediacy. Your offering should feel like the key that fits perfectly into the lock of the present moment.

Monitoring and managing ad spending can feel like walking a tightrope. However, with Facebook's robust analytics, you have a safety net. Allocate budgets based on results—not just on gut instinct. Start small and scale up only those adverts that demonstrate a healthy return. Always be nimble, ready to pivot and reallocate resources as needed, to those ads delivering results that make your accountant smile.

Ever noticed how a handshake feels warmer when it's personalized? In the realm of digital advertising, retargeting is that personal touch. It's a strategy designed to re-engage folks who have already shown interest in your product or service. Crafting exclusive offers for them increases the likelihood of conversion. After all, they've already been in your store, so to speak; now you just need to help them find the checkout counter.

Fresh out of the gate, many ads may stumble. Perseverance, paired with the fine-tuning of ad elements, is what separates winners from the rest. Success in Facebook advertising doesn't come overnight; it's brewed over time through a cycle of testing, learning, and evolving. Each campaign is a learning experience, a stepping stone to understanding your audience better and serving them more efficiently.

The power of storytelling in your ads can't be overemphasized. Every ad you create should like a mini-drama that entices your audience to stay tuned. Pull them into a narrative that leads them on a journey ending with your product or service as the hero. Everyone roots for a good story. Be a compelling storyteller and watch engagement soar.

Your ad's landing page—it's the crescendo of your symphony. A disjointed landing page experience is like hitting a sour note that threatens to ruin the entire piece. The transition from ad to landing page should be seamless, and the landing page itself should fulfill the promises made in the ad. It's a continuation of the journey, and it should lead inexorably towards that final commitment—be it a purchase, a sign-up, or a download.

As your ad campaigns run their course, they accumulate vast swathes of data. Harness this data to gain insights into customer behavior and preferences. Use these insights to tailor future campaigns even further, thus entering a virtuous cycle where each ad outperforms the last. This is listening to what the numbers are telling you, and it's an exercise that can drastically improve your returns.

Community engagement often goes overlooked in the quest for sales. Engage with those who interact with your ads. Respond to comments, answer questions, and cultivate a sense of community. An engaged community is more likely to invest in what feels like their own. This is the intersection of customer service and marketing—a place where loyalty is born and brand ambassadors are made.

Automation tools and third-party integrations are friends to your Facebook ad efforts. They can help streamline processes, align your ads with email campaigns, manage leads more effectively, and provide richer analytical insights. By leveraging technology, you can manage campaigns with the precision of a Fortune 500 company, without being one—yet.

Finally, even if Facebook is a colossal cornerstone of your digital marketing efforts, don't operate in a vacuum. A holistic approach, integrating your Facebook ads into a wider digital marketing strategy, yields the best results. Your ads should be a part of a larger conversation happening across various platforms and mediums, all converging on your ultimate goal of skyrocketing your business's value.

Remember, the essence of maximizing return on Facebook ads is a vibrant blend of creativity, strategic analysis, and an unwavering focus on results. Every ad dollar spent should be an investment in your company's future, positioned towards that glamorous goal of a 10X exit. With smart, adaptable strategies, your Facebook ad campaigns can be a powerful lever to pull your business above and beyond your most ambitious benchmarks.

Leveraging Google Ads for Growth As we turn the pages from maximizing returns with Facebook advertising, let's shift our focus to an equally compelling avenue: Google Ads. It's a platform where potential customers are actively seeking what you offer. Imagine placing your business at the apex of that search, harnessing intent and converting it into growth. Those over 50 running a business often have wisdom and experience on their side, but may not be harnessing the full potential of digital tools like Google Ads. It's high time to change that.

Google Ads is not just a marketing platform; it's a growth accelerator waiting to be tapped. At this stage in your business journey, you're aware that mere presence in the market isn't enough. It's about visibility—being in the right place at the crucial moment when a potential customer decides they need what you're selling. And this is where Google Ads shines. It allows you to target those who are already looking for solutions you provide, reducing the gap between demand and supply with the precision of a skilled archer.

The beauty of Google Ads lies in its flexibility and measureability. You can tailor ads down to the minutest details—keywords, location, demographics, and even time of day. This level of customization ensures your message reaches the right people at the right time, without spraying resources into the void. Remember, targeted reach isn't just efficient; it's cost-effective, reducing wastage and increasing your return on investment.

Think of Google Ads as a dynamic agent in your sales process. You can use it to run campaigns that tackle different stages of the customer journey. From awareness to consideration to the final decision, there's a type of campaign for every phase. Through search campaigns, display ads, video ads, and even shopping ads, you're covering a spectrum of touchpoints, making your brand hard to overlook.

Now, let's talk skyrocketing your growth—literally. Did you know using Google Ads effectively can position your business above organic search results? This premium placement is like putting your store on the busiest street corner, only it's the digital highway we're bustling on. It's visibility at its peak, a tool that can drive high-intent traffic straight to your doorstep.

Constructing the perfect ad campaign is akin to painting a masterpiece. It begins with understanding the finer nuances of keywords. These are the seeds from which your Google Ad campaigns will blossom. Investing time into meticulous keyword research ensures you're not blindly casting a wide net, but spearfishing for high-quality leads that are far more likely to convert.

On crafting your ads, clarity and relevance take center stage. In an age where attention is the greatest currency, your ads need to capture and hold it within moments. Simplify your message, highlight your unique value proposition, and always, always make sure your call-to-action is irresistible. An effective call-to-action turns the passive observer into an active participant, stepping into your well-crafted sales journey.

Another critical factor in leveraging Google Ads is the art of bidding. Say goodbye to guesswork; Google's bidding strategies are designed to match your specific goals. Looking to enhance brand exposure? There's a bid strategy for that. Want to drive more site visits or increase conversions? Google Ads has bid strategies for those objectives as well. Master the bidding to control spend and maximize outcomes.

Now, a whisper of caution—a mighty tool wields no power without control. Google Ads has a vast array of features and learning how to navigate them with precision is key. Don't be daunted by the complexity. You've navigated more challenging waters in your years at the helm. Take it one step at a time, starting small, testing, learning, and refining as you go.

Moreover, don't let your ad campaigns set sail and forget about them. The digital sea is ever-changing. Regular monitoring and adjustments are not just recommended; they're crucial. Analyzing the performance data helps you understand what's working and what's not, allowing you to pivot swiftly and effectively. This constant optimization process ensures you're not just growing but growing smart.

To maximize the yield from your Google Ads, align them with your sales funnels. The messages in your ads should offer seamless transitions into the various stages of your funnels. This cohesive strategy builds trust and encourages progression from one step to the next, smoothly guiding your prospects closer to conversion.

Integration doesn't end there. Google Ads should be a part of your larger digital marketing ecosystem, working synergistically with your SEO efforts, content marketing, and online sales funnels. Such integration ensures a cohesive online presence, driving home your message from multiple angles and touchpoints, increasing the chances of conversions.

As we look towards skyrocketing your growth through Google Ads, remember that your return on investment is paramount. While it's easy to get caught up in vanity metrics like clicks and impressions, focus on the numbers that translate to true business growth—conversions, customer acquisition costs, and customer lifetime value.

And to those who worry that the technological leap might be too wide— fear not. The brilliance of technology today is that it can be tailored to suit your capabilities. There's a wealth of resources at your fingertips, from support teams to instructional videos, ensuring that the tech empowers rather than overpowers you.

By effectively leveraging Google Ads, you aren't just gambling on chance —you're engineering growth. You're setting sail into a digital ocean with wind in your sails, ready to catch the trade winds of the internet era. It's time to take the wheel, steer your business towards uncharted territories, and harness the full potential of Google Ads to not just grow, but to grow exponentially. Because when it's time to exit, you won't just want a profitable sale, you'll want a monumental one. A 10X exit. And Google Ads is your gateway to that destination.

Integrating Online Sales Funnels acts as a bridge that directly connects you to the heart of digital opportunity. Think of it as the magic in the beans, the map to the treasure. You've learned the power of digital marketing, but now, let's pivot to how you can take full advantage using online sales funnels to not just grow, but explode, the value of your business.

First things first, set aside any apprehension you may have about adapting to new technologies. Remember, at its core, an online sales funnel is simply a systematic approach for guiding someone from not knowing about your business to becoming a loyal customer. And guess what? It's a process that's been in practice long before the internet was even a twinkle in the world's eye.

Now, the crucial step is to create a funnel that resonates with your customers' needs. Consider your target audience—their pains, problems, and desires. A well-crafted funnel speaks directly to these points, offering solutions at every ledge of the dive down into the funnel's depths. It's not about bombarding an audience with ads, it's about providing value and leading them through a journey where the natural conclusion is to engage with your business.

Incorporating an online sales funnel requires an intimate understanding of the customer journey. Break down the walls of confusion by mapping out this journey step by step. From the moment they land on your website (thanks to those laser-focused Facebook and Google Ads, right?), your funnel must clearly guide them towards the action you want them to take, whether that's making a purchase, signing up for a newsletter, or requesting more information.

Emails, they're like the personal messengers cycling through your funnel, whispering the right words at the right time. Utilize them wisely as they're your surefire tool to nudge those sitting on the fence, rally the troops if you will, with tailored messages that tap into their individual situations.

Remember, the fastest path to a sale is trust. A funnel infused with testimonials, case studies, and guarantees lifts the veil of doubt. Picture it as embedding layers of rock-solid, unwavering trust with every click they take, assuring them that they're making the right choice with each commitment.

But wait, there's more to this tale. You've no doubt heard of landing pages. These aren't just random pages on your website; they're the swords arming your funnel, designed to convert. Craft each page with a specific purpose in mind, honing in on one call-to-action that rings louder than any belltower. It's not about overwhelming prospects with options; it's about guiding them to that one action that'll transform them from a visitor to a customer.

Now, let's touch on analytics—the epitome of funnel fine-tuning. Imagine you're sailing; analytics are your compass, guiding you, showing where the winds of customer behavior are blowing. Track everything—the clicks, the time spent on each page, the conversion rates. These aren't just numbers; they're the bread crumbs leading you back home to what works and what doesn't.

As your business scales, you'll find that automation is your best friend. What once was done manually, like sending out those crafty emails or updating customer records, can now be done with elegance and efficiency, giving you more time to focus on what you do best—growing your empire.

The beauty of a well-oiled sales funnel is also in its ability to upsell and cross-sell. With each step, offer products or services that complement their journey. It's about increasing your average order value, nudging them to consider not just one product, but a few others that might pique their interest.

Think about the lifetime value of a customer. It isn't just about that first sale. Oh no, it's about fostering an ongoing relationship. Your sales funnel should be designed with this in mind. Create follow-up sequences, loyalty programs, and ways to keep in touch. It's about making every customer feel like they're the hero in their own story, with your business as the sage guide illuminating the path forward.

Now, let's shift gears and talk about content because, in this digital age, content is king. Your funnel is the path, but your content is the scenery along the way that keeps them walking down it. Be it blog posts, videos, podcasts, or infographics—each piece should serve a purpose, either to educate, entertain, or convert. It's this content that keeps the connection between you and the customer alive and kicking.

What about the technical side, you ask? Websites, CRM systems, payment gatekeepers—they're foundational bricks of your online funnel fort. Partner with platforms that integrate seamlessly, ones that serve as reliable pipelines connecting you to your customers without leaking precious opportunities.

Lastly, don't forget the humanity behind the screen. Each interaction in your funnel, be it automated or manual, should feel as personal as a handshake. It's not about replacing the warmth of human contact; it's about enhancing it with the efficiency and scale the digital realm allows.

The bottom line is clear: an online sales funnel is a tool of transformation, a builder of bridges between potential and prosperity. With it, you'll not just attract eyes; you'll nurture hearts and minds that believe in what you offer. And when the day comes to step away, you'll be leaving behind a business ripe with value—ready for a tax-free exit that's just as strategic as the journey that brought you there.

As we venture further into the land of opportunity and strategy, keep your sales funnel at the forefront of your mind. It's not just a piece of the puzzle; it's a master key unlocking levels of growth you've yet to imagine. Your journey is one towards legendary success, and the integration of online sales funnels is a powerful steed to help you gallop towards that horizon.

Chapter 3: Social Media Mastery

Following our deep dive into the transformative power of digital marketing, let's shift our lens to the energetic world of social media—a realm where customer engagement and brand presence can ignite your business's influence and set your revenue streams on fire. Social media isn't just for the tech-savvy youth; it's a goldmine for seasoned business owners determined to cast a wider net and capture hearts across generations. This chapter isn't about aimless scrolling or frivolous posts; we'll sink our teeth into dynamic strategies to command YouTube's algorithm, weave the rich tapestry of your brand narrative across Facebook and Instagram, and even ride the wave of TikTok's viral tendencies without losing a shred of your distinguished brand identity. It's time to master these digital domains with precision and intention, transforming your social platforms into engines of exponential growth. With a well-cobbled social presence, you can build a fortress of loyalty around your customers, not only amplifying your business's valuation but also crafting a narrative that's irresistible when the time comes to exit—tax-free and on top of the world.

Strategies for YouTube Success Now, let's dive deep into the powerhouse that is YouTube—an arena where visuals and storytelling collide to create a potent platform for business growth. Imagine harnessing the world's second-largest search engine to catapult your business into the spotlight, leveraging a medium where billions of eyes are glued, ready to be captivated by your brand's story. In this section, we'll explore the strategies that can turn your YouTube channel from a mere presence into a formidable force that drives your business's value skyward.

First, let's establish a crystal-clear objective. Your YouTube channel should not be a random collection of videos; it needs to be an orchestrated campaign that funnels viewers into customers, and customers into loyal advocates. Clarify what action you want viewers to take after watching each video: should they sign up for a newsletter, visit a landing page, or perhaps check out a new product? Laser-focused intentions breed resounding outcomes.

Next, content is king but consistency is key. Develop an intentional posting schedule and stick to it. Whether it's weekly, bi-weekly, or daily, a regular cadence creates an expectation and builds a habit in your audience. They'll know when to tune in for fresh insights, creating a rhythm to their engagement with your brand.

But what about the content itself? Craft narratives that resonate. You're not just selling a product or service; you're providing a solution to a pain point, an enhancement to your customers' lives. Create content that educates, entertains, and inspires. This cements your brand as a valuable resource within your industry.

Quality can't be compromised. You're in a competitive arena, after all. Investing in good lighting, clear audio, and professional editing pays dividends. It's a reflection of the excellence you stand for—don't skimp on the details that elevate your brand above the fray.

Engagement is the currency of social media, and YouTube is no different. Encourage interaction by posing questions, prompting viewers to comment, and, most importantly, responding to those comments. This dialogue creates a community around your channel, fostering loyalty and increasing the likelihood that your content will be shared.

Don't underestimate the power of optimization. Your videos need titles, descriptions, and tags that not only captivate but also align with what your target audience is searching for. Like a beacon, SEO helps guide potential viewers through the vastness of YouTube to your channel's shore.

An often overlooked aspect is the importance of a compelling thumbnail. It's the first impression viewers get. Make sure it's clear, high definition, and contains an element—be it text or an image—that makes someone want to click through.

A robust channel is one that's plugged into a network. Collaborate with influencers and other businesses in your niche. These partnerships can amplify your reach and lend additional credibility to your brand. Identify potential synergy and explore how team collaborations can result in a multiplicative effect.

Measure, refine, repeat. Without analytics, you're sailing without a compass. YouTube provides robust tools to understand who's watching, from where, and why they're engaging—or not. Tuning into this feedback loop allows you to make data-driven decisions that refine your strategy over time.

Bring your offline efforts online. Your business events, customer testimonials, and behind-the-scenes insights provide a wealth of content opportunities that showcase your brand's personality. Share these moments, and let your audience see the human side of your business. This transparency builds trust, endearing your brand to viewers.

Don't forget the Call to Action (CTA). Every video should compel viewers to take a step further into your business orbit. Whether that's visiting your website, signing up for an exclusive offer, or following your brand on other social platforms, make it seamless for them to connect with you in multiple ways.

Leverage YouTube ads as a catalyst for accelerated exposure. With targeted advertising campaigns, you can zero in on your ideal demographic and deliver your message straight to their screens. It's a strategic push that can dramatically increase your channel's visibility and direct quality traffic your way.

Keep an eye on the future. As you build a repository of content, start thinking about evergreen videos that continue to provide value over time. This is the type of content that works for you indefinitely, constantly bringing in new viewers and maintaining relevance regardless of season or trend.

Finally, patience and persistence are your allies. Your channel might not explode overnight, but with a steadfast commitment to these strategies, growth is inevitable. It's about planting seeds today that will bloom into a thriving garden of opportunity that elevates your business for that 10X exit.

With these strategies in hand, you have the blueprint to transform your YouTube channel into a dynamic engine of growth for your business. Visualize the end goal, craft your story, invest in quality, foster community, and continuously adapt. Do this, and watch as the digital waves propel your brand towards that horizon where a prosperous exit awaits, yes, tax-free and gloriously magnified.

Building a Brand on Facebook and Instagram is not just about posting photos and waiting for likes to roll in; it's an art form, a strategic play, and an essential piece of your business's growth puzzle. Here, we're peeling back the curtain on the approach that can put your business in the spotlight, engaging an audience that's eager to stand behind your brand and, ultimately, add zeros to your business value.

First off, envision your brand as a personality, a character in the grand narrative of the marketplace. Every post you make, every story you share, should resonate with the essence of this character. Don't hold back; infuse your brand's voice in every interaction. Your authenticity will shine, captivating exactly the audience you seek.

Content is king, but consistency is the key to the kingdom. Your posts should be frequent and regular, creating a rhythm that keeps your audience engaged and expecting more. This consistency isn't just about when you post, but also how reliably your content reflects the core values your business stands for. When your followers know what to expect, they build a trust that's tough to shake.

Engagement begets engagement in the interconnected world of social media. When your followers comment, take the time to reply. Create content that invites conversations and community input. Your responsiveness shows that there's a caring human behind the brand, and that can make all the difference in fostering loyalty.

Facebook and Instagram flourish on visuals—bold, eye-catching images and videos that stop users mid-scroll. Invest in high-quality visual content tailor-made for each platform. Remember, what works on Instagram's image-driven platform might not resonate on Facebook's more varied content ecosystem.

Metrics are your map through the digital landscape. Both platforms offer robust analytics to help you understand who your audience is, which posts resonate, and when your audience is most active. Use this data to refine your strategy continually. It's not just about the numbers; it's about understanding the story those numbers tell.

Cultivating a community doesn't stop at your business's virtual doorstep. Partner with influencers and brands that align with your values to extend your reach. These collaborations can introduce you to whole new audience segments who could become your most ardent supporters—and future customers.

Advertising is a potent tool on both platforms, allowing granular targeting that gets your message in front of the right eyes. But throwing money at ads isn't enough; craft your campaigns to speak directly to the aspirations and needs of your potential client. Be clear on the action you want them to take and make it as straightforward as possible to go from discovery to conversion.

Stories and live videos are the spice that keep your feed fresh. These fleeting glimpses give your audience a sense of immediacy and insider access. Don't shy away from these tools; use them to showcase the behind-the-scenes of your business, spotlight special offers, or share flash sales that create urgency.

Hashtags may seem like a small detail, but they can widen your content's visibility significantly. They're not just for show; think of them as beacons that guide like-minded individuals to your page. Use them wisely and with intent, focusing on those that are trending but still relevant to your message.

User-generated content is a treasure trove of authenticity. It's one thing for you to praise your product, but when customers share their love for what you offer, it's social proof gold. Encourage your followers to tag your brand and share their experiences. Celebrate these posts by featuring them on your page, which can motivate even more customers to join in.

Exclusive deals and competitions can stoke the excitement and incentivize engagement. Use your Facebook and Instagram presence to offer something special for your social media followers, creating a club-like feel that makes following your brand a valuable proposition.

Remember, while Facebook and Instagram are pillars of social media branding, one size doesn't fit all. Tailor your content and approach for each platform. Instagram's visual-driven environment might be perfect for showcasing products, while Facebook's community groups could be just the place to build deeper discussions and brand loyalty.

Rise above the noise of the digital sphere by crafting a narrative for your brand that's compelling, relatable, and share-worthy. Your story is the thread that connects customers to your brand, making them a part of something greater than a transaction. It's that sense of belonging and connection that can transform casual followers into lifelong customers and brand evangelists.

So, let's look past the simple goal of increasing followers and likes; instead, aim to build a thriving community that stands the test of time. When the time comes for you to make your graceful exit, you'll find that your authentic, engaged, and passionate social media presence has not only amplified your immediate profits but has also exponentially increased the value of your brand in the eyes of prospective buyers. And when you sell? You sell a brand that's alive, loved, and ready to continue thriving without you at the helm—that's the 10x difference.

Harnessing the Viral Nature of TikTok is akin to catching lightning in a bottle. But let me tell you, it's a storm worth chasing for your business. When we talk about magnifying the value of your business and exiting with a sum that feels like winning the lottery tax-free, you can't ignore the digital colossus that is TikTok. This platform's meteoric ascent isn't just for the trendy teens – it's where future fortunes are minted.

Imagine propelling your brand into the spotlight with a single, well-orchestrated video. It's not just plausible, it's happening daily. TikTok thrives on the new and the now, and its algorithm loves to serve up content from all creators, irrespective of their follower count. That's an open invitation to you – business owners – to grab a slice of this vast attention pie.

The first step is to understand TikTok's currency – and that's creativity and authenticity. Your business need not dance to the latest hit, but you must move to the rhythm of what captivates your audience. Content that resonates on a visceral level, content that makes them laugh, think, or drop their jaws, is what skyrockets to virality. Your mission is crafting messages that stick.

Diving into TikTok marketing, think not solely about promotions but about storytelling. Each post should be a chapter that adheres cohesively to your brand's narrative, one that educates or entertains but always aligns with the greater tale of your company. Stories are the hooks that can make your brand unforgettable, with TikTok as your stage.

To truly leverage this platform, care immensely about timing and trends. TikTok's heartbeat is quick, powered by the pulsing of trending sounds, challenges, and hashtags. Your business should tap into these movements, to be a player, not a spectator in the race for virality. Aligning with trends gives your content a tailwind, propelling it forward.

Yet, don't let the fear of perfection paralysis stop you. TikTok endears itself to the real, the raw; it celebrates imperfection. When producing content, yes, ensure it's high-quality, but don't get bogged down in a never-ending pursuit of flawlessness. Often, immediacy trumps perfection. So shoot, share, and fine-tune as you go.

Engagement on TikTok isn't a one-way street. It's a bustling highway of two-way interactions. Responding to comments, duetting with fellow users, participating in challenges – these are goldmines for engagement. A brand that listens, interacts, and appreciates its community galvanizes supporters into ambassadors.

Understanding your audience is paramount. What do they crave? What can your business uniquely offer? Utilize TikTok analytics to drill deep; know when your audience is online, what they engage with the most, and tailor your content to these insights. It's about merging your expertise with their interests, forming a potent mix that captivates.

Cover all bases by diversifying your content. As fascinating as your product may be, an endless stream of product videos grows stale. Inject tutorials, behind-the-scenes peeks, customer testimonials, or even slices of your business journey into the mix. Show the multifaceted diamond that your business is.

Let's talk about hashtag usage. Hashtags are not just appendages to your content; they are conduits connecting your videos to a broader audience hunting for that specific content. Research, utilize, and even create branded hashtags that anchor your content in the vast ocean that is TikTok.

Collaborations are a linchpin of TikTok success. Partner with influencers who echo your brand values, who have the trust and the ears of your potential customers. Shared content with these TikTok mavens is like an endorsement megaphone, bolstering your credibility and reach exponentially.

TikTok ads too, offer a profitable avenue. They can complement your organic efforts, catapulting your brand into target feeds with precision. Invest wisely, track performance, and iterate your ad campaigns for optimized results. Paid strategies when done well, can work in tandem with organic growth, creating a virtuous cycle of brand amplification.

Embrace the fleeting, test relentlessly. Launch a content piece, analyze its performance, and use the insights to sharpen your TikTok darts. The more you test, the more you understand what makes your audience tick (or TikTok). It's a process of constant learning and adaptation, iteratively inching closer to that viral hit.

But remember, TikTok is just one piece of a grander strategy. It's a tool in your arsenal for 10X-ing your business's value. Integrate it with your other digital marketing efforts; let it feed into your sales funnels, complement your Facebook and Instagram strategies, and reinforce your overall brand ethos.

As you journey on this exhilarating TikTok adventure, stay grounded in your brand's core mission. Venture boldly into the trends, but never lose sight of the values and the vision that mark the cornerstone of your business. With the right strategy, creativity, and a splash of tenacity, your TikTok presence can be a pivotal chapter in your 10X growth story.

Dare to make waves in this dynamic digital sea. Your business story deserves an audience of millions, and with TikTok's viral nature at your fingertips, you're well on your way to scripting a success saga for the ages. The world's stage awaits, and it's your time to shine.

Chapter 4: Explosive Growth Through Acquisitions

Imagine your business, as you know it, suddenly doubling or even tripling in size—yes, not over years, but in an afternoon. That's the towering potential of growth through acquisitions. For savvy business owners who've mastered their market, this isn't some high-stakes gamble; it's a calculated, strategic move that can redefine your playing field. We've touched on revolutionizing your digital reach and social media presence, but now, let's shift gears to a move that can ignite growth at a pace you've only dreamed of. By deftly picking and integrating businesses that align with your vision, you're not just adding to your portfolio; you're multiplying your capabilities, expanding your customer base overnight, and drastically increasing your market share. It's about transforming your company into a powerhouse with the leverage to command your industry and sculpt a legacy. In your golden years, this is how you build an empire resilient enough to not only withstand the test of time but to flourish in ways that will leave even you in awe. Envision your closing chapter not as a farewell but as a grandiose finale—your business's value spectacularly magnified, setting the stage for an exit that's nothing short of monumental and, yes, tax-free. Let's dive into this exhilarating journey of growth, and I'll guide you through the art of kingdom-building, one acquisition at a time.

Doubling Your Business Size in an Afternoon

Imagine the atmosphere if you could amplify your business size like the growth rings of a mighty oak—but in just an afternoon. It sounds mythical, yet it's possible with one of the most potent maneuvers in the business playbook: acquisitions. Let's expand on what you know about growth and tap into the celebrated power of smart acquisitions.

First up, it's crucial that we differentiate between organic growth—an admirable goal that's linear and often painfully slow—and the growth that comes from acquisitions. When you acquire, you aren't just adding; you're multiplying your capabilities, your market share, your team, and potentially, your bottom line.

Growth through acquisitions requires a shift in mindset. You're no longer nurturing a single tree but planting an entire forest. By incorporating a well-matched business, you can double your size virtually overnight. Sounds exhilarating, doesn't it? Because it is. But this is not a leap into the unknown, it's a calculated progression.

The reality is, businesses just like yours have done it. They've found a compatible company and wrestled with the numbers, the strategy, and the integration. Proper due diligence is non-negotiable. We can't just point to any business and claim it as our growth ticket. We need to find the right fit with the right fundamentals. It's like matchmaking—with a thorough background check.

Why acquisitions though? Because once you're past the 50-year mark, time takes on a different meaning. While the value of patience is well-understood, the allure of acceleration cannot be ignored. You've got the wisdom to know what works, and now, you're looking to scale that impact, quickly and significantly. Acquisitions can cater to that urgency.

To start, you'll need to recognize businesses that are ripe for the picking. These might be complementary services or products that can seamlessly dovetail with your current offerings. Or, it could be a competitor that's been struggling, yet has a loyal customer base or perhaps a geographic foothold you've eyed for years.

Next, the financials. This isn't about splurging on a business like it's a weekend splurge at your favorite golf shop. The acquisition must make financial sense. Crunch those numbers, forecast the growth trajectory, and ensure your capital is working smarter, not just harder.

But finance is only the beginning of the picture. Culture is key. A business clash can cause a promising deal to crumble into dust. It's paramount to consider how the teams will meld. Will your visions for the future align or will they clash like titans?

Then, there's the operational dance. You've built systems that work like a well-oiled machine. How will another company's gear fit into the engine you've so meticulously tuned? Ensure compatibility, or at least have a robust plan for integration.

When you have these components aligned, negotiation enters the stage. If you're not careful, this could be where the plot twists. It's a delicate balance between assertiveness and empathy, between value extraction and value creation.

The signature on the dotted line, while a thrilling moment, is just the precursor to the true work: integration. This is where the vision of doubled business size translates into operational reality. This phase is daunting but crucial; it's where many acquisitions falter or flourish.

Post-acquisition, monitoring performance and tweaking the machine are essential. This isn't the time for pride if things need pivoting—better to swallow the medicine now than to suffer indigestion later. Smart, swift adjustments can mean the difference between an acquisition that soars and one that sinks.

And lest we forget, amidst the hustle of deals and dollars, this isn't just about the numbers; it's about people, too. An acquisition might double your business size, but it also brings aboard more hands to share the workload, more brains to innovate, and more hearts to invest in your collective vision. This human element is where true growth potential resides.

Let's not sugarcoat it—the road of acquisitions has its share of potholes. However, with a keen eye for opportunity, a shrewd mind for negotiation and integration, and a bold heart for the human side of business, the promise of doubling your business in one fine afternoon isn't just a daydream—it's a very achievable reality. A reality that will catapult your exit value through the stratosphere, positioning you for that tax-free sale that will secure your legacy.

Remember, the expansion of your empire need not take a lifetime. So, heed this invitation to consider acquisitions as your secret weapon, the powerful catalyst that can redefine your business horizon in the span of an afternoon. The opportunity is out there, waiting for the seasoned glance of a business sage like yourself to seize it. Will you take the leap and watch as your business blossoms exponentially before the day is through?

Navigating the Acquisition Process So you've strategically grown your business, and now you're considering an acquisition as a turbo boost on your journey to a 10X exit. That's an exhilarating step forward! Acquisitions can seem complex, but with the right mindset and a structured approach, you can steer through this process with finesse and confidence. The goal here is not just to acquire, but to do so in a way that profoundly escalates your business's value, leaning into a seamless, profitable exit strategy.

Firstly, remember that a successful acquisition starts long before you approach a potential target. It begins with clarity. Be razor-sharp about what you're looking for in a company to acquire. Are you aiming to expand your product line, enter new markets, or maybe add a technological edge to your operations? Ensure your objectives are aligned with your ultimate goal of increasing the value of your business. You're looking to create that perfect synergy where one plus one doesn't just add up to two but much more.

Next up, let's talk valuation. Determining the right price for an acquisition is part science, part art. It requires a thorough analysis of the target's financials, understanding their market position, and evaluating potential for future growth. But don't get lost in the numbers. Consider the less tangible assets, like brand strength and customer loyalty. These can be just as crucial to your 10X journey as the balance sheet.

Due diligence is your best friend. It's about digging deep and getting to know every inch of the target company - warts and all. You're not just buying their successes; you're also buying their challenges, so understanding these is key. Don't rush this phase. The more thorough you are, the better positioned you'll be to make a smart acquisition that won't leave you with unwelcome surprises down the line.

Financing your acquisition is another major step. There are multiple paths you could take—from traditional bank loans to seller financing or even leveraging your existing assets. Think creatively and analyze which option will best serve your growth strategy while maintaining healthy cash flow. It's not just about seizing an opportunity; it's about doing it wisely without compromising the financial stability you've worked so hard to build.

Integrating an acquired company into your existing operations is no small feat. It's a delicate dance that, if done well, can lead to a spectacular routine. Consider cultural fit – your employees and theirs need to mesh well, embracing change and driving the newly combined entity towards common goals. This cultural integration is as critical as meshing together IT systems or financial reporting.

Retaining key talent post-acquisition can be a game-changer. The people who made the acquired company successful can be instrumental in a smooth transition and continued success. Engage with them early, communicate your vision, and demonstrate how they play an integral role in the future of the united businesses. People drive performance, so make sure they're on board and in the loop.

Communication throughout the acquisition process cannot be overstated. It is vital to maintain transparency with your stakeholders - employees, investors, customers, and the newly joining members from the acquired company. Regular updates and openness help to build trust, reduce uncertainty, and ensure everyone is pulling in the same direction toward that golden 10X goal.

While navigating the legal landscape, it's best to have a formidable team by your side. Lawyers, accountants, and financial advisors who have seasoned experience in acquisitions will prove to be invaluable. This team will help you cross every 't' and dot every 'i', ensuring your deal not only looks good on paper but also stands the test of times.

Post-deal, your work is only beginning. Acquisitions should be followed by decisive action – aligning systems and processes, consolidating operations where it makes sense, and pushing forward with renewed vigor towards your growth targets. Remember, momentum is key. Keep your foot on the pedal and your eyes on the horizon.

On the topic of future growth, ponder the scalability of your new, enlarged enterprise. Now that you have more resources, how will you maximize them to further amplify your growth trajectory? This is critical because the value of your business at exit will be proportional not just to your current earnings but also to your potential for expansion.

Assessing risk and having contingency plans in place is essential. In an acquisition, not all will go according to plan. Risks range from cultural misalignment to missed financial targets. Prepare for such instances by developing strategies that safeguard your core business without stifling the growth potential of your new asset.

Leveraging the acquisition for market positioning is a savvy move. Use the strengths of the acquired company to bolster your brand's visibility and standing in the marketplace. This strategic move can result in increased market share and customer base, and ultimately a more substantial, more attractive business when it comes time to sell.

The ultimate gauge of a successful acquisition is how it propels you towards your exit strategy. Keep an unwavering focus on the endgame – a tax-free, lucrative exit. How does this acquisition get you closer to that? It should fortify your business, making it resistant to competition and ripe for a premium offer from prospective buyers.

When the time comes to exit, the narrative of your acquisition journey will be compelling. It will be a story of strategic growth, operational excellence, cultural integration, and visionary leadership. This narrative can significantly influence the perceived value of your business in the eyes of buyers, potentially commanding a premium price.

Lastly, celebrate the milestones. Acquiring a business and navigating it towards a 10X future is no mean feat. Celebrate the small victories along the way with your team. These moments of recognition fuel the drive towards your ultimate goal. The journey towards a monumental exit is peppered with challenges, but with determination, savvy decision-making, and a great team, the path is clear. Your tenacity will be rewarded, and the legacy of your business will be the monument of your successful entrepreneurial journey.

Chapter 5: Scaling High-Impact Face-to-Face Sales

As we shift gears from digital prowess to the art of personal connection, let's dive into how you can scale high-impact face-to-face sales. In the flesh, a handshake has more electricity, and a direct gaze carries more conviction than any pixelated image could ever convey. Remember this—your most potent sales tool is the ability to connect, to listen, and to solve problems on a personal level. Imagine multiplying that effectiveness across an army of your best salespeople. It's about building trust at scale, systematically expanding your reach while maintaining the warmth of personal connection. Because at its core, business is not B2B or B2C; it's human to human, H2H. At this stage in your business journey, you already know your worth, your product's superiority, and the value of shaking hands with precision and intent. Your mission now is to cast this knowledge wider, to empower a fleet of relational magicians—AKA your sales force—who can mirror your passion and personality. They'll be your lighthouses, guiding ships laden with profits safely into your harbors. So let's unlock this treasure chest together, transforming every prospect's nod into a yes, and every yes into a ripple that reverberates across the waters of your industry. The tools and tactics are here for you to seize; let's ensure your message doesn't just echo—it roars.

Leveraging Your Contacts for Maximum Revenue taps into a goldmine that's been right under your nose all this time. Let's dive in, shall we? Your contact list isn't merely a collection of names and phone numbers—it's a treasure trove of relationships, each with its own unique potential to skyrocket your revenue. It's about playing the long game, shaping these relationships into partnerships, client deals, or even sources of referrals.

Firstly, have a look at that list with fresh eyes. Remember, these are not just contacts; they are individuals who know your worth, trust your experience, and have potentially seen your business flourish over the years. They respect your hustle and share a connection with you that's built on years, perhaps decades, of mutual respect.

It's critical to value each contact as a personal relationship rather than as an abstract opportunity. Relationships drive business in today's world, and yours are ripe for nurturing. The key is personalized communication. Tailor your messages, offer assistance, and be genuine. Pick up the phone. Have a conversation. Building these connections can transform them into recurring revenue streams.

Assess the strength of your relationships. Some contacts may know what you're capable of but may not know what you're offering right now. Use this as an opportunity to update them—not through a sales pitch, but as part of a natural catch-up. People enjoy doing business with those they're familiar with, and a friendly update can lead to new ventures.

Strategic introductions can be potent. If you're in a position to make connections between contacts who might benefit from each other's services or collaboration, you become a valued resource—a central hub in your network. As you facilitate these introductions, your contacts are likely to reciprocate in kind, introducing you to potential clients and opportunities.

Also, take advantage of client testimonials. There's a natural inclination to take pride in our work, but there's incredible power in others singing your praises. Collect glowing endorsements from your existing contacts and display them where potential clients can see. This amplifies trust, stokes curiosity, and can be the tipping point for a new customer choosing you over a competitor.

Let's not forget about exclusive offers. Everyone likes to feel special and your established contacts are no different. Give them first dibs on a new service, or a discount on an existing one. This not only gives them an incentive to engage but also to share the offer with others in their circle who might need your services. One contact's interest can snowball into a flurry of business before you know it.

Host events, even virtually, that add value without a sales pitch. Webinars, workshops, or networking events can provide priceless opportunities to reconnect with contacts. By providing value first, without asking for anything in return, you plant the seeds for future revenue. Plus, these events give you a chance to dazzle them once again with your expertise.

Understand the art of the follow-up. It is not just a courtesy; it's a business maxim. Many deals aren't struck at the first meeting, or even the second. It's those consistent, value-driven follow-ups that build the kind of trust which leads to transactions. Keep the lines of communication open and follow up with an aim to provide solutions, not just to sell.

Consider creating a contact loyalty program. We're not talking about a mere discount card but a full-fledged recognition of their loyalty to your business. Maybe it's an annual event exclusively for long-term clients or a specialized service tier. This attention to their business makes your contacts feel acknowledged and can spur them to contribute even more to your bottom line.

And then there's the power of upselling and cross-selling. Your existing contacts might be familiar with a segment of your offerings but remain unaware of your full suite of services. Educate them on how they can benefit from your other products or services. The ones who already believe in your business are the most likely to expand their patronage.

Don't forget to reward referrals. If a contact sends new business your way, show your gratitude in a tangible way. Whether it's a discount, a gift, or a public shout-out, acknowledging their support encourages a continuous cycle of referrals. It's a small investment for potentially large dividends.

Stay ahead of the curve. Keep your contacts informed about industry trends or new insights. By positioning yourself as a thought leader, you ensure that they turn to you when they're ready to take advantage of these new market opportunities. This keeps you relevant and at the forefront of their minds.

Finally, remember to listen. As you interact with your contacts, pay close attention to their needs and challenges. This attentive approach not only aids in tailoring your offerings but also in creating new ones that address their specific circumstances. By being a business ally that solves problems, you solidify your essential role in their professional lives.

Tapping into the inherent power of your contacts for maximum revenue isn't about manipulation or a hard sell. It's actually about mutual benefit, trust-building, and being genuinely invested in seeing your contacts succeed. With this approach, you're not just increasing revenue; you're also creating lasting loyalty and a robust, supportive business network. Your contacts aren't just entries in a database; they are vibrant partnerships just waiting to be deepened. Forge ahead, and watch your business—and theirs—thrive like never before.

Building Personal Rapport and Closing Deals picks up where leveraging contacts left off, transforming raw leads into enduring business relationships that don't just generate a sale today but pave the way for that monumental tax-free exit tomorrow. It's about the profound impact of person-to-person connections in a world swamped by digital interactions. One authentic conversation can outweigh a hundred emails.

Building genuine rapport isn't as hard as it seems—it's about being present, attentive, and most importantly, genuinely interested in the other person. Your approach has to convey more than a superficial charm. People can sense when you're going for the hard sell, and it often sends them running. Give them a reason to stay, show them that their success is your success.

When you engage with potential buyers, it's critical to come from a place of service. Ask questions and actually listen to the answers. It's not merely about the responses you get, but the trust you build by showing you care. When you understand their challenges and goals, you're not just selling them something—you become the ally that can help them overcome and achieve.

Remember, synergy is more potent than the sum of individual efforts. When you connect with clients or partners, it's like a dance. It takes two to tango, and you're not leading solo. This synergy is about aligning your strengths with their needs, creating mutually beneficial outcomes. That's when deals close almost effortlessly and value multiples because it's rooted in real partnership.

Imagine upping your emotional intelligence to the point where it acts like a sixth sense—tuning into subtle cues and adjusting your pitch without missing a beat. It's this level of attunement that distinguishes those who close deals from those who merely push them. People want to feel understood, not handled. They want to make a decision with you, not be sold to.

So elevate your conversations. Talk about the vision, the big picture. How does what you're proposing fit into their dream of growth and success?

When they can see their business blossoming with your offering as a cornerstone, the doors to closing deals swing wide open.

Storytelling is another powerful tool at your disposal. It's one thing to tell someone what your product can do; it's another to show them through a story that resonates. The psychological impact of a well-told tale, relevant to their context, can break walls and build bridges. A story can make your pitch memorable and shareable long after you've left the room.

When it comes time to closing, finesse is key. This isn't about applying pressure; it's about guiding your potential client to the edge of decision and empowering them with confidence to leap. Confirmation bias is your ally; once someone starts leaning in your direction, gently reinforce their thought process with affirmations and evidence. It's not trickery; it's facilitation.

Of course, the nitty-gritty cannot be ignored. Know your numbers and be prepared to discuss the return on investment. Business owners are won over by hard data as much as they are by soft skills. It's not just about making them feel good about the deal; it's about showing them it makes sense in bold, unambiguous figures.

Remember, your attitude is contagious. If you're passionate and optimistic about the prospects of the deal, that energy can be persuasive. But beware of overconfidence; it can come across as insincerity or lack of authenticity. Striking the perfect balance between assurance and humility is like finding gold.

Follow-up can't be an afterthought. It's the pulse that keeps the relationship alive post-meeting. A thoughtful email, a check-in call, or a useful article are all touchpoints that say 'I'm still here, and I'm still invested in your success.' That resonance keeps you at the forefront of their minds even as they navigate a sea of daily business distractions.

Locking in the deal is the beginning, not the end. It's a commitment, not just to the sale but to the relationship. That's where the doors to referrals and future ventures open. A deal is a jigsaw piece to a much larger puzzle —the potential of a business relationship that can flourish and expand.

Finally, always remember to show gratitude. Whether a deal is made or not, acknowledging the time and effort involved strengthens your professional character and leaves a lasting impression. Gratitude creates a thread of warmth and respect that people remember—and it's often what brings them back to the table.

The craft of building personal rapport and closing deals is as much art as it is strategy. Own it, and you open a world of possibilities. It's about connection, endurance, and the profound impact of leading with humanity in a business landscape. With each deal, you're not just inching toward a 10X valuation; you're creating a ripple of relationships that could define your legacy.

Let this section be the springboard into a more profound understanding of the human factors at play in business growth. It's how you turn transactions into relationships and relationships into a flourishing enterprise. It's the handshake before the digital age, the eye contact in a world of screens, the personal touch that says you're more than a business owner—you're a visionary building an empire of value and values.

Chapter 6: Streamlining Operations for Efficiency

As we pivot from mastering direct sales into revamping internal gears, Chapter 6 keys into creating that seamless, well-oiled machine every business owner dreams of. The secret's out: trimming excess fat from operations isn't just about cutting costs—it's about shooting for the stars in productivity and setting a pace that competitors can't match. Think of it as tuning up a classic car; you want every part humming in harmony. It's about smarter, not harder work, where automation technology isn't a buzzword but your right-hand man in beating the clock and slashing those overheads. By refining processes and embracing technological aides, you're crafting an avalanche of efficiency ready to snowball into bigger profits. This chapter isn't a deep-dive into every nut and bolt but giving you the map to spot efficiency bottlenecks and the tools to clear them fast. You'll see how streamlining becomes the rocket fuel for that coveted 10X business value—and how operational finesse sets you up for an elegant, tax-free exit curtain call.

Creating a Smooth-Running Operation Understanding this concept is critical for addressing the challenge ahead—you've set your sights on boosting business value, and now you're paving the road to a smooth transition. Smoothing out your operation is less about avoiding all turbulence and more about being able to quickly recover your balance when you hit an unexpected bump. It's about resilience, grace under pressure, and a robust set of systems that can withstand the trials of scaling and acquisition pressures.

Imagine your business as a well-oiled machine. Each gear turns in synchrony with the others, interlocking with precision and purpose. That's what we're aiming for—a business where every component is optimized for both efficiency and preparedness. Ensuring that your operation runs like clockwork starts with deep knowledge of your processes, a commitment to continuous improvement, and fostering a productive work environment where everyone knows the part they play.

Now, drill down into the essence of your workflow. Take a hard look at the nuts and bolts—where are the friction points? Where does the process slow down or choke under pressure? By identifying these areas, you're not just troubleshooting; you're unearthing opportunities for profound growth and efficiency gains. That's because, often, the biggest roadblocks hide the greatest opportunities for exponential improvements.

Empowerment is the catalyst for a smooth operation. Equip your team with the right tools and authority to make decisions that align with the overarching company goals. Ensure that everyone has access to information that affects their work. Transparency isn't just a buzzword; it's the linchpin of operational efficiency. When your team has clarity on the 'why' behind their actions, they're more likely to take initiative and drive productivity.

Streamlining communication isn't just about fewer emails; it's about major-league effectiveness. There's an art to ensuring that messages aren't just sent but also received and understood. Cultivating an environment where communication is clear, concise, and constructive creates a foundation for quicker resolution of issues and better teamwork. This doesn't happen overnight, but with persistence and practice, you will see dramatic positive changes in how your team operates.

Every operation has its set of repetitive, energy-draining tasks. Automation is your friend here. Jump on the tech-train and don't look back. Identify the time-consuming processes that can be automated, and introduce software solutions that can handle them with greater accuracy and speed. This frees up your invaluable human capital to focus on more strategic, growth-driven activities, rather than getting bogged down by the mundane.

Remember, a smooth operation is also about expectations. Set realistic timelines and deliverables that account for the human element in your business. When your team has clear targets and sufficient time to hit them, they're empowered to work with increased vigor and determination. This is where your leadership shines, guiding them toward that target with vision and support.

Dive into data analysis. Your operations are a goldmine of actionable insights. Continuous monitoring and evaluation of performance metrics help pinpoint inefficiencies and successes. Cultivate a data-driven culture where decisions are based on evidence and analytics, not just gut feelings. When your entire operation is aligned with key performance indicators, you can steer the ship towards success with precision.

But a smooth operation isn't just about productivity; it's also about maintaining it during rapid growth or unexpected setbacks. To achieve this, you must be proactive. Develop contingency plans for potential obstacles and market fluctuations. When you prepare for the unexpected, it's easier to maintain composure and continuity when faced with challenges.

Don't neglect the personal development of your workforce. Investing in your team's growth equates to investing in your operation's efficiency. Provide training opportunities that enhance their skills and foster a culture of lifelong learning. An equipped and educated workforce is more adaptable and can manage the intricacies of a complex operation with dexterity. Plus, it sends a powerful message: Your growth is the company's growth.

Meticulous financial management is also pivotal. Be astute with your financial resources, ensuring that cash flow is managed effectively. In a smooth-running operation, fiscal responsibility is not optional—it's core to survival and scaling. Develop budgets that reflect both the immediate and future needs of your business, keeping an eye towards strategic investments that will drive your 10X vision.

Quality is your silent ambassador. Regular quality checks and controls must be embedded into every thread of your operation. Consistent quality builds trust with your customers, reduces waste and inefficiencies, and cements your reputation. The quality of your product or service is the bedrock upon which you'll amplify the value of your business.

Consider also the physical aspect of your operations. Your working environment impacts productivity and employee satisfaction significantly. Create a space that encourages focus, creativity, and wellbeing. This could mean optimizing layout for workflow efficiency, establishing 'green' areas for mental breaks, or ensuring ergonomic furniture is available. Respecting and enhancing the physical workspace pays dividends in operational efficacy.

And finally, adopt a mindset of iterative improvement. Your operation should never truly be 'finished'. A culture that values feedback and is always seeking out the 'better way' is one that is constantly moving forward, pushing boundaries, and finding new ways to thrive. Encourage suggestions from all levels of staff and remain receptive to change. The most successful operations are those that evolve organically with the industry and customer needs.

Creating a smooth-running operation is about synthesizing these elements into a coherent, well-functioning whole. It's about precision, but also about fluidity. It's cultivating an environment where your business not only operates seamlessly but also adjusts and thrives amid change. When you master this, you're setting up your company not just for a 10X future, but also for a tax-free exit that rewards you for all the careful crafting of an operation that runs like a dream. So, take the wheel with confidence and know that with each small adjustment, you're driving towards a future of incredible potential and prosperity.

Implementing Tech to Automate and Enhance Workflow is comparable to giving a craftsman state-of-the-art tools; it can significantly enhance productivity and product quality, both of which can drive your business's value through the roof. We're in an age where leveraging technology isn't just an option; it's a necessity if you're aiming to 10x the value of your business and ensure a lucrative, tax-free exit when the time comes for you to move on.

When we talk about implementing tech, it's not about jumping on every digital bandwagon. It's about using the right kind of technology to sharpen what your business does best. Imagine having portions of your business running smoothly with minimal oversight, giving you more time to focus on strategic growth. Automation is that silent engine in the background that makes this possible.

Dive into your operations. What repetitive tasks are eating into your team's time? It could be as simple as data entry or scheduling. These are prime candidates for automation. There's software out there that can take these off your plate, reducing errors and freeing up your team to engage in more value-added activities. Streamlining these workflows with technology can not only save you time but also dramatically cut costs in the long run.

Opting for a Customer Relationship Management (CRM) system transforms how you handle your contacts and leads. With a robust CRM, follow-ups, and lead nurturing becomes automated, consistent, and personalized. Your sales team's productivity can skyrocket because they're no longer bogged down by manual tracking. They're doing what they do best: closing deals and forming personal connections that basic tech just can't replicate.

Let's not forget the power of cloud-based collaboration tools. They've been game-changers, letting teams work together from virtually anywhere. As business owners, we should be harnessing these tools to enable on-the-go productivity and ensure that information is always at our fingertips. Why let geography limit your talent pool or your productivity?

Now, you might be thinking, "This tech stuff sounds expensive." But here's the thing – the return on investment can be mind-blowing. Automation technologies often come at an upfront cost, but calculate the hours saved and the efficiency gained, and you'll see a sizeable increase in margin over time. A CRM, for instance, could seem like a significant initial investment, but the increase in conversion rates and customer retention will more than makeup for it.

For those who fear the potential complexity of implementing new tech, there's plenty of user-friendly software that's designed with a gentle learning curve in mind. And let's not ignore the immense support and resources available; from online tutorials to dedicated customer service – adoption has never been easier.

Not investing in automation and tech can also mean leaving money on the table. If your competitors are embracing these efficiencies and you're not, it's akin to racing with ankle weights. Remove those weights, and you'll be surprised at how much quicker you can run.

Integrating an online project management system can keep your entire team aligned with real-time updates and visibility into each other's tasks and deadlines. This eliminates the endless back-and-forth emails and meetings that can drain time and energy – two resources that are far too valuable to waste when you're gunning for exponential growth.

The notion of workflow automation may seem impersonal or detached, but that's a misconception. When you automate routine tasks, you're actually enhancing the human element of your business. You're enabling your team to devote more time to innovating, engaging with customers, and improving your product or service. It's technology at the service of humanity, not the other way around.

Let's not brush aside the significance of data analytics. Employing technology that can analyze trends and predict customer behavior is like having a crystal ball at your disposal. This insight allows you to make data-driven decisions quickly, staying ahead of market curves and often, your competitors.

But remember, the implementation of technology should be strategic. It isn't just about having the latest gadgets and gizmos. Each piece of technology needs to serve a specific purpose and align with your broader business goals. As a decision-maker, you have to ensure that the tech complements your business, rather than complicates it.

Remember, this isn't just about today's gains. Future-proofing your business by staying abreast of relevant technologies lays a strong foundation for your eventual exit. A business that runs like a well-oiled machine, with efficient automated processes, is far more attractive to potential buyers or investors. They're not just investing in your current profitability; they're investing in the sustainability and scalability of your operations.

In conclusion, embrace the change. Let tech take on the grunt work so you can unleash the full potential of your business and your people. Implementing tech to automate and enhance workflow isn't just a fancy option; it's essential for scaling up, increasing value, and ultimately securing that tax-free exit you've set your sights on. It's time to let technology work its magic on your business, carving out the path for a future where your enterprise thrives beyond your hands-on involvement.

So, think about your business processes. Which aspects could run themselves with the right tech in place? The sooner you integrate technology into your workflow, the quicker you'll push your business toward that 10x horizon. And the beautiful part? You'll have more time to craft the future you envision, both for your business and for your life after the exit.

Chapter 7: Systems and Processes: The Backbone of Scaling

In the journey we've embarked on, we've identified the high-octane fuel for our engines – acquisitions, digital marketing, social media savvy, and salesmanship – and now it's time to talk about the structural integrity of our vehicle: systems and processes. Think of it, if our business is a towering tree, our underlying systems are the roots gripping the earth, holding everything steady enough to shoot sky-high. This is the chapter where we unveil the secret sauce that holds empires together, pushing past that critical threshold where many plateau. It's not just about working harder but smarter, leveraging every ounce of effort for maximum output. You'll soon discover that while genius might get you started, it's the repeatable, efficient systems and the fault-tolerant processes that help you scale, sustain, and ultimately, secure that golden ticket to a lucrative exit. Hang tight, because we're about to turbocharge your business infrastructure, ensuring that as you aim for a 10x multiplier, you've got the relentless, unwavering support of a foundation engineered to withstand the exhilarating climb to the summit of entrepreneurial success.

Why You Can't Scale Without Them

You've got a vision for where you want to go. That's great, but a vision without a solid foundation is like a skyscraper with shaky stilts—it's bound to come crashing down. The cornerstone of that foundation? Systems and processes. These aren't just flow charts and manuals gathering dust; they're the living, breathing scrolls that dictate how your empire operates. Without them, you cannot scale. Period.

Think of it this way: you wouldn't build a house without a blueprint, right? Systems and processes are your business's blueprint. They're what enable you to duplicate success repeatedly across different areas of your business, free up your time, and assure quality control. They are the unspoken heroes of consistency, and consistency is king in the world of scaling up.

Maybe you've got stellar sales techniques or a product that's second to none. But guess what? Without a process to produce and sell that product efficiently, your growth will plateau. Systems allow you to take that winning formula and replicate it across teams, locations, and markets. Without them, you're a one-hit wonder, but with them, you become the seasoned artist with a portfolio of hits.

It's not just about what you're doing today, but also about what happens when you're not around. Scaling means growth without your day-to-day involvement. Systems and processes allow your team to make decisions and respond to challenges in ways that align with your big-picture goals. It's like having a mini-version of you in every department, making sure your vision stays the course.

We live in a golden age of technology, where automation and software can take on much of the heavy lifting. Implementing tech to automate your processes isn't a nice-to-have; it's a must-have for scaling effectively. It cuts down on error, streamlines communication, and keeps the cogs turning smoothly and swiftly.

Scaling is not just about growing in size—it's about growing sensibly. Your operations need to be lean and mean, and that's where optimizing systems and processes make all the difference. When you make tweaks to improve efficiency, you're essentially increasing your capacity to take on more business without a proportional increase in headaches or overhead costs.

But here's the rub: developing and refining these systems can't be an afterthought; it has to be intentional. It takes patience and persistence to create a process that works and then optimize it to perfection. But once that's done, it frees you up to focus on strategy and innovation—the very things that got you into business in the first place.

Every time you avoid reinventing the wheel, you save time, money, and gray hairs. This is why documentation is essential. Detailed records of your processes make them transferable knowledge rather than tribal knowledge. It ensures that the why and the how of your business methods aren't locked in any one person's head.

Let's face it; employee turnover is a reality. With well-documented systems in place, you can bring new hires up to speed quickly, ensuring minimal disruption to your growth trajectory. No need for a panic when a key team member takes a vacation or, dare I say, moves on. Your business won't just survive; it thrives because the system runs the show, not the other way around.

Moreover, when you have these systems down pat, scaling geographically becomes a viable option. Imagine replicating your business model in a new market. Without a tried-and-true process, it's a gamble. With it, you've got a roadmap for success that's been tested and proven in the trenches.

And let's not forget the power of a process in negotiation: when it comes time to exit, having robust systems in place makes your business infinitely more attractive to buyers. They're not just buying your revenue; they're buying the machine that guarantees that revenue. It's like the difference between buying a treasure map and an actual treasure chest full of gold—it's a no-brainer.

Lastly, through the lens of scale, processes also mitigate risk. With clear procedures, you minimize the chance of errors that can cost time, relationships, and yes, money. It's about protecting your investment by being as fail-safe as possible. You wouldn't leave the door to your house wide open when you leave, so why leave your business exposed?

In sum, you can't scale without them because systems and processes are more than the nuts and bolts of a business—they are the essential framework that supports and enables sustainable growth. They give your team the autonomy to succeed, your operations the efficiency to expand, and your future plans the clarity they need to blossom into reality.

Now, you might be itching to jump straight into the details of developing and optimizing your business systems but hold that thought. This book walks you through how you can build the right structures in place, step by step, ensuring that when you do scale, you do it with confidence. After all, a steady hand builds the strongest empires, and yours is well on its way to stand the test of time.

As you turn the pages and absorb the insights, remember this: systems and processes are not just back-office stuff. They're the engines of your ship, powering you through uncharted waters with resilience and poise. Embrace them, and you'll not only reach your destination but enjoy the journey, too.

Developing and Optimizing Your Business Systems is integral to your journey towards a colossal exit—one that not just meets but exceeds all your aspirations. Imagine your enterprise as a powerhouse where every gear and lever operates in sublime harmony. This isn't a dream; it's what your business can be with fine-tuned systems. Step by step, let's unlock this potential together. You've got the experience—now let's amplify it with precision.

Think of your business as a beautiful watch. Every piece crucial, from the smallest cog to the elegant face it presents to the world. Systems are the cogs in your company. When optimized, they work silently and efficiently. They allow you to delegate with confidence, knowing that your business will not just survive, but thrive, in your absence. It's this kind of self-sustaining operation that's attractive to buyers and what will ultimately drive up the value of your business.

To optimize your business systems, start by mapping them out. Not just what you think they are, but how they actually operate in the real world. Dive in, get your hands dirty, and scrutinize every routine and process. This in-depth understanding is crucial for pinpointing areas that need refinement or complete overhaul. You're the master and commander, and this ship sails at your command—make sure every route is charted for smooth sailing.

Next, focus on automation. You've seen technology evolve over your career; now embrace it fully. Intelligent software isn't just a convenience —it's a game-changer. It takes routine tasks and completes them faster and with fewer errors than any human could. This transformation isn't just about cost savings; it's about elevating your team's focus to where they make the biggest impact—in creative thinking and personal service. Harness tech to handle the mundane so that your human talent shines in exceptional service and innovation.

Now, let's hone in on existing protocols. Are they gold mines of efficiency or relics of bygone eras? It's time to reimagine them with a kind of relentless pragmatism. Keep what works, refine what's rough, and discard the rest. Your processes should flow like a river—naturally and powerfully toward your ultimate goal. Each team member becomes a steward of this flow, trained to not just perform tasks but to seek continuous improvements.

Measurement is your compass here. It's not enough to implement a system; you must track its performance. Define clear metrics for success and scrutinize the data like it's the secret to El Dorado—because it just might be. Regularly reviewing these metrics means you're not just expecting success; you're demanding it at every turn. And when something's off-course? You'll be on it, fine-tuning with the precision of a master craftsman.

Communication within a well-oiled business machine can't be overstated. Every member of your team should understand not just the how, but the why of their actions. Connect the dots between each role and the overall success of the company to foster a sense of ownership and purpose. Let's make this personal, because when your team is genuinely engaged, they're not just working for you, they're working for the shared triumph.

Empower your team to take the wheel. Cross-training and delegating authority means your business doesn't falter when you're not at the helm. This shows potential buyers that the company's success isn't hitched to any single star—it's a constellation of skilled professionals taking joint ownership of their roles. It's about building a company that's more powerful than the sum of its parts.

Redundancy isn't a dirty word; it's a security blanket. What happens if a system fails? Have backups, have plans B, C, and D. Contingencies that mean when the unexpected hits, your business doesn't just stand resilient, it continues to excel, unshaken. This robust foundation isn't just comforting; it's a hallmark of a mature enterprise, one that runs like clockwork come rain or shine.

Let's talk innovation. You aren't just maintaining systems; you're driving them forward. Encourage innovation at every turn. Allow your team the space to suggest and implement improvements. Celebrate the wins and learn from what doesn't work. This culture of constant enhancement propels your business forward, molding it into an entity that's not just surviving the market—it's shaping it.

Don't forget, it's not just about internal operations. Your customer service systems need to be stellar. Elevate customer interactions from necessary to memorable. Streamlined, delightful experiences that have clients not just returning, but raving. Fanatic about your service, they'll be the megaphones propelling your reputation far and wide. It's this kind of word-of-mouth that can't be bought; it's earned, one ecstatic customer after another.

Training is where the magic happens in system optimization. It's not a one-off, it's a culture. A culture of learning, development, and mastery where you invest in your team so they can invest their skills back into your business. As they grow, so does the quality and consistency of their work—and by extension, your company's output. It's a virtuous cycle, really—a rising tide lifting all ships.

So, you've got the right systems and team in place—what's next? You need to maintain this ecosystem. Regular check-ins and system audits keep things humming. Identify not just the issues but the potential—you're on the hunt for opportunities to get better, sleeker, and more profitable.

Finally, document everything. Clear, comprehensive documentation means that your finely tuned engine keeps purring even when key players are no longer on the scene. It's not enough to know your business inside out; your systems should be a canvas, clear for any successor to pick up the brush and continue the masterpiece.

Remember, every step you take to develop and optimize your systems brings you a notch closer to that stunning exit. You're not just building a business; you're crafting a legacy. One that lives on in the excellence it delivers, the jobs it supports, and the wealth it creates. This is your magnum opus. Make it count.

With the gears of your business turning smoothly, you can now look forward. The right systems are in place, primed to elevate every other aspect of your enterprise. You've created a fortress of efficiency and innovation, now let's see what flag you'll fly from its towers.

Chapter 8: Building and Retaining a Stellar Management Team

Let's think big. Your business isn't just a vehicle for today's profits; it's your legacy and your massive payday waiting to happen. Imagine a management team that isn't just good but stellar—a team that drives your business forward, that embodies and executes your vision, making your company irresistible to buyers and multiplying its worth tenfold. It's about identifying leaders who see what you see, dream what you dream, and possess the drive to shoulder responsibilities with savvy and zeal. Crafting such a team isn't happenstance; it requires a keen eye for talent, a nurturing hand to grow potential into excellence, and a steadfast commitment to an environment that retains these game-changers. You'll foster a place where management thrives on autonomy while aligning seamlessly with company goals. Reflect on the insights we've shared so far – from digital dominance to mastering social media, through to strategic acquisitions, face-to-face sales dynamism, operational efficiency, and system supremacy. All these empowering components are potentiated by a management team that doesn't just adapt but takes charge, innovating and propelling your business toward that 10X valuation. Remember, a stellar team is the keystone for a fortress of success—build and strengthen this team, and you're not just setting the stage for your grand exit, you're ensuring an enduring legacy that thrives even in your entrepreneurial sunset.

Identifying and Cultivating Leadership Talent In the thrilling journey of ramping up your business's value, a pivotal chapter often overlooked is the cultivation of leadership within your ranks. Remember, the strength of your leadership team can make or break your ability to scale and, ultimately, to achieve that dream of a 10X exit. A gem doesn't shine without polishing, and the same goes for your leadership talent. It's about spotting those rough diamonds within your organization and rigorously refining them until they sparkle.

Step back for a moment and picture your enterprise not just as a business, but as a fertile ground for growing leaders. You've got experience on your side, a treasure trove of insights only time can bestow. Use that wisdom to identify those with a glimmer of potential. Pay attention to not just the performance, but the character, the resilience, the ingenuity that surfaces in moments of challenge. This task is not a sidebar—it's a central piece of the puzzle in amplifying your business's value.

Once you've identified those with potential, it's time to get your hands dirty in the cultivation process. Leadership is not just about directing a crew; it's about inspiring, problem-solving, and innovating under pressure. Provide your budding leaders with opportunities to stretch— give them projects that push their limits and watch how they grow. But remember, growth often comes with growing pains. Support them, coach them, and offer feedback that's as nourishing as it is challenging.

It's not enough to throw your potential leaders into the deep end and hope they swim. Development is a process, a journey you need to guide them through. Invest in leadership training—programs that mold not just skills, but mindset. Believe in the power of mentorship. Your experience is gold; share it. Pair your rising stars with seasoned veterans, and let the fusion of energy and expertise forge your future leaders.

This cultivation should happen at all levels. Instill leadership qualities in your teams from the ground up. Everyone should know how to take the helm when the seas get rough, regardless of their title. Cross-training, rotational assignments, involvement in strategic meetings—these are the seeds of versatility and leadership in your employees. By doing so, you're not just preparing individuals to lead; you're preparing your business to withstand any storm.

Ask yourself, what's the point of growth if it isn't sustainable? You want leaders that will carry on your legacy, your ethos, who can navigate the ship to success even when you're sunbathing on some tropical shore post-exit. Invest in creating a leadership manual, a tome of wisdom that distills your approach to business and leadership into a guide your leaders can turn to.

But let's get real—leadership isn't just about giving orders; it's about garnering respect and cultivating relationships. Encourage your leaders to connect, to understand the unique motivations of each member of their team. People will work wonders for a leader they trust and believe in, so mentor your leaders to be approachable and empathetic.

Don't forget to celebrate the wins, both big and small. People thrive when their efforts are recognized. A shout-out, an award, a company-wide email of praise—simple acts that resonate deeply. Recognition fuels the drive to excel and affirms that one is on the path of true leadership.

Consider the legacy you want to build. Your leaders are your immortality in the business world. How they lead, how they drive success, how they inspire—it all begins with the seeds you plant today. So be deliberate in crafting a leadership development plan that aligns with the vision and values you hope to perpetuate long after your exit.

Movement matters. Keep your leadership pool dynamic; encourage internal mobility. Leaders exposed to different areas of your business gain a holistic understanding that's invaluable. They'll see the puzzle, not just the pieces, and that comprehensive insight is what drives a company forward in a way that's both innovative and grounded.

Never underestimate the power of feedback. Encourage your leaders to seek it actively, not just from their superiors but from their peers and their teams. Leadership is a performance, and every performance can be tweaked, improved. Embrace a culture where feedback is the breakfast of champions, consumed daily to nourish one's leadership capabilities.

Remember, your leadership team is your frontline in the battle to scale. They're the torchbearers of your culture, strategy, and operational excellence. So allocate resources for their development as you would in any critical business operation. Think of it as investing in the very infrastructure of your business's future.

One final, crucial piece of advice: never stop searching for talent. Leadership isn't static; it evolves as your business does. Keep an eye on the horizon for individuals that bring something fresh to the table. Be willing to bring in outside talent if necessary to complement and challenge your existing leadership framework. New blood can stimulate growth, catalyze innovation, and inject a sense of urgency that stirs the competitive spirit within your ranks.

As you ascend to that coveted 10X exit, ensure your leadership is ascending with you. They're not just executing your vision—they're amplifying it, they're personalizing it, they're the ones transforming it from idea to reality. Cement your legacy, not just in the annals of history, but in the thriving, vibrant culture of leadership that propels your business tantalizingly close to that 10X finish line.

So there it is, the blueprint to spin straw into gold, to transform your keen-eyed, ambitious employees into the leaders who will share in carrying your banner towards that hilltop of success. It's in people that we invest, and it's people who repay that investment tenfold, a hundredfold, when they rise to become leaders who drive your business—and its value —sky-high. The pursuit of a tax-free exit begins and is sustained by the strength of your leadership team, so focus there and you've set the stage for a grand finale that will be talked about for generations to come.

Empowering Teams for Autonomy and Success You know the value of a stellar team. It's the engine under your business's hood, the human horsepower driving your company toward that 10X horizon. But let me throw you a curveball: A team's prowess isn't just in its collective strength —it lies in its autonomy. Give your team the reins, the right tools, and the clear 'why' of your business's mission, and watch success unfold.

You began with visioning a future, understanding exit goals, and gauging your company's worth. You delved into the digital realm, social media, and you've started mastering the dance of acquisitions. Now, we're shifting gears to fortify the core of our business machine: our teams.

To fuel explosive growth, a strong, autonomous team is not just a nice-to-have, it's a must-have. Just think, every minute you're not solving a problem, it's being handled by someone who's empowered, trained, and ready. That's what true autonomy can mean for your team—and for you.

But how do we get there, you ask? It starts with trust. Yes, the 'T-word'. Trust your people. Hire individuals brighter than a Fourth of July fireworks show, and then trust them to deliver. It's about crafting positions that allow them to make decisions, to run with projects, and to take ownership of their results. Micromanagement? That's the old-school, tie-and-suspenders way that'll choke your business growth quicker than you can say 'paper jam.'

Let's talk empowerment. And no, I'm not just talking about cheerleading from the sidelines—true empowerment is arming your team with the decision-making power they need to excel. That means giving them access to resources, finances, and the autonomy to make judgement calls that align with your overall vision and strategy.

And with empowerment comes accountability. Create a culture where outcomes, not just effort, are celebrated. Outcomes are the fuel for your business, the very stuff that propels you forward. When your team takes ownership of their goals, hat drops become high-fives, and setbacks become setups for better solutions. It's about aligning their successes with those of the business—when they win, everyone wins.

Communication is the golden thread holding this tapestry together. It's not just about talking, it's about connecting dots. Clear expectations and a shared understanding of the bigger picture ensure that your team is rowing in the same direction—and with gusto.

Now, you may fret over potential mistakes. You're not alone. But consider this: mistakes forged in the fires of autonomy become lessons that stick. They become the hard-earned wisdom that can turn a greenhorn into a seasoned navigator in the choppy seas of business.

Creating self-sufficient teams also allows you, the captain of the ship, more time to scout the horizon. This isn't about stepping back; it's about stepping up to strategize, innovate, and chart the course forward. While your crew manages the sails, you're steering toward that fabled tax-free exit.

Let's also address scalability. A self-empowered team is a scalable team. When your team can manage, sell, and innovate without a constant from-the-top push, you're set up to multiply your business size without being bogged down in day-to-day operations. This isn't just growth; it's sustainable, exponential, and the kind of scalability that primes a business for acquisition—big league style.

Investment in leadership development is non-negotiable. You're a talent scout in the big game of business. Find the spark plugs, the go-getters, and then invest in them. Supply them with the leadership skills, the coaching, and the room they need to expand into dynamic, autonomous leaders themselves.

Remember, this isn't just delegating tasks; it's delegating outcomes. We're not talking 'complete X by Thursday.' We're talking 'improve X by 10% within the quarter.' And then you let them pilot the ship to that destination, in the manner they deem best, as long as it sails true to your company's North Star.

Finally, remember the human element. Your team is not made up of robots. They've got goals, dreams, and desires. Connect with them. Understand those motivations and harness them. When their personal aspirations align with your business goals, that's when the magic happens. It's the seamless intertwining of purpose, passion, and productivity that creates an unstoppable force.

There you have it, your blueprint for building a team that's not just functional but phenomenal. A team that's not waiting for orders but is out there making a splash, delivering value, and setting the pace in your industry. That's how you solidify your legacy and position your company as a dominator in the marketplace, primed and ready for that spectacular, tax-free curtain close when you decide it's time to take the bow.

Remember, empowering your team for autonomy isn't just a tactic, it's a transformation. It's an approach that fundamentally changes the way your business operates, lays the foundation for unprecedented growth, and sets you up for a grand, graceful exit. Now, isn't that a future worth building towards?

Chapter 9: Crafting a Positive Company Culture

As we pivot from the complexities of building a strong management team in Chapter 8, it's crucial to recognize that the essence of your company's prosperity lies in the heart of its culture. Think of culture as your business's DNA—it's something that permeates every aspect of your operations, influencing your team's mindset and behaviors. Attuning to a positive and productive company culture doesn't just echo in the present; it reverberates into the future, setting the stage for a business that blossoms and can amplify its value tenfold. Embedding core values that resonate with your vision and mission doesn't just skyrocket efficiency; it magnetizes the right talent and retains them. It's the secret sauce that fosters engagement, sparks innovation, and drives a 10X growth trajectory. So let's roll up our sleeves and sculpt a workplace atmosphere that's not just a mere place to work, but a vibrant community pulsing with enthusiasm and dedication—a place where everyone rowing the boat is not only in sync but ecstatic about the direction you're heading. As we unpack the strategies to infuse your culture with this transformative energy, remember, it's this pivotal shift that can catalyze an empire and usher in a lucrative, tax-free exit on your terms.

Driving 10X Growth with a 10X Culture taps into one of the deepest veins of human potential within your business. You've seen companies abound with energy, passion, and a collective drive that seems almost palpable. That's no coincidence. It's the result of a deliberately cultivated 10X Culture where each person feels empowered to contribute to the grand vision. This isn't about kumbaya moments at company retreats; it's about embedding a growth mindset into your organization's DNA.

Think about it — you can have all the strategy and resources in the world, but without a team that's as invested in your business's growth as you are, you're running a one-man show. Now, let's picture a workplace where every individual comes in burning to shatter ceilings, transcend boundaries, and multiply outcomes. That's your 10X Culture.

Start with why. Simon Sinek had it right; when people understand the why behind their work, they're far more likely to take ownership of it. The key is to communicate a compelling vision, clear and bright as day, so every team member not only understands the direction but is also excited to push toward it.

What's next? Priority alignment. It's not just about being busy; it's about being busy doing the right things. Your culture should celebrate the deeds that drive the needle, not just activity for the sake of activity. It's the difference between a rocking boat and one that's surging ahead. To build this, you have to model it — prioritize relentlessly and help your team do the same.

Consider communication as the bloodstream of your culture. It's got to flow, uninterrupted, nourishing every part of your business with information, ideas, and feedback. Open the channels, encourage honest dialogue, and watch as ideas collide and coalesce into something greater.

But what about the inevitable barriers? Silos. They can stifle growth faster than a dam cuts off a river. So break 'em down! Cultivate interdisciplinary teams that are encouraged to work out loud. Transparency isn't just about honesty; it's about enabling everyone to see the big picture and find their fit within it.

And let's not skip over recognition. Imagine the fire it adds to a person when their efforts don't just get a nod but a fireworks show of appreciation. Recognize the wins, big or small, and you fuel the motivation engine of your organization. It's this kind of reinforcement that turns effort into exponential results.

However, it's not all sunshine; there's room for failure in a 10X Culture. It must be understood as tuition paid for learning. When you destigmatize making mistakes, you empower your team to take calculated risks — and that's where innovation thrives.

With that said, a 10X Culture isn't just built on the wings of freedom. It's also structured with accountability. Your team must know that, while the sky's the limit, there are solid expectations grounding their work in reality.

And don't forget about talent — your glow-in-the-dark, rock stars. They may be few, but their impact is tenfold. Invest in them, develop their skills, and watch them act as catalysts for culture and growth. As they improve, the ripple through your organization can turn into a tidal wave of growth.

Now imagine all this culture shaping geared not just towards a healthy workplace, but also towards preparing your business for that tax-free exit. Yes, a 10X Culture goes hand-in-hand with multiplying your business's value. When people are smashing goals as a collective, your numbers don't just climb; they leap.

But it all starts with you. The leader, the visionary — your mindset is the primer for your business's exponential journey. Like a master gardener, nurturing a field that will one day yield an abundant harvest, you've got to plant the seeds of growth, tend to them, and sometimes prune boldly. Set a standard of excellence and passion that makes average seem like a forgotten concept.

Implementing a 10X Culture necessitates that you too are willing to go beyond. You can't expect what you don't inspect. Be there, in the trenches, leading the charge. Remember, the energy of the leader is the energy of the pack.

And yes, this transformation is achievable. Start small if need be, with consistent daily practices that, when compounded over time, will craft an environment so potent in its ability to grow your business, you'll wonder why you ever settled for less.

Let's land on this — a 10X Culture is not a nice-to-have; it's an essential driver of 10X Growth. It's about cultivating an environment that doesn't just enable but amplifies success. It's the secret sauce that turns businesses into legacies, and ordinary exits into tax-free windfalls. So, plant the seeds today, nurture them well, and prepare for the harvest of a lifetime.

As you turn the page, remember, a 10X Culture is the soil in which a 10X future is grown. Your efforts today toward building this culture are the most potent investment in your business's extraordinary tomorrow. Let's harness the power of your team to multiply their impact, your growth, and ultimately, the legacy you leave. It's time to live and breathe the essence of 10X.

Implementing Core Values for Company Alignment Picture this: you're standing at the helm of your business, and ahead lies the immense potential of a 10X future. You've envisioned it, strategized for it, and now it's time to align every facet of your company with that vision. This alignment is where core values become the compass that guides your ship, keeping it steadfast during the tumultuous journey towards significant growth and a lucrative exit.

Core values aren't just words slapped on a wall or a website; they are the lifeblood of your corporate body. Imagine them as the DNA that defines who you are as a company, what you stand for, and how you act in the business world. They are not to be taken lightly. Forging and implementing core values demands introspection, sincerity, and commitment, quite like laying a foundation that'll bear the weight of the empire you're set to build.

Let's begin by clearly identifying core values that resonate authentically with your vision. This requires you to dive deep - what beliefs and principles have been the bedrock of your success so far? What moral and ethical lines would you never cross, regardless of the potential profit? Identifying these values unearths the unshakeable truths at the heart of your business. These truths will be your North Star, steering you through decisions, partnerships, and strategies as you scale up.

Once you've identified your core values, it's time to weave them into the very fabric of your company. They should be evident in every process, every interaction, and every decision. This means revisiting your operations, from customer service scripts to product development life cycles, ensuring they all reflect your company's values. It's not just about the 'what' of your business but also the 'how'; the way you operate should be a mirror image of your core principles.

Communication plays a critical role; it's not enough to know your core values - your team needs to live and breathe them too. It's essential to articulate these values clearly and frequently. Create a narrative around them, tell the story of why they matter and how they've driven the company forward. This builds a sense of shared vision and purpose, integral to fostering a unified culture among your team.

But don't stop at just talking the talk; you have to walk the walk. Demonstrate how these values guide your decisions by leading by example. If one of your core values is 'customer commitment', go above and beyond in resolving a customer's problem – then highlight how this aligns with your values. Over time, these actions set a powerful precedent, establishing expected behaviors within your team.

Recognizing and rewarding behaviors that exemplify your core values reinforces their importance. When an employee goes out of their way to align their actions with the company's principles, shine a light on it. Celebrate these wins and make them as public as possible. It's about creating heroes in your organization that embody the values you hold dear, thereby inspiring others to follow suit.

Embedding your values into hiring practices is crucial as well. You need people who not only have the skills but also the character to mesh with what your company stands for. During interviews, tailor questions to gauge the alignment between a candidate's personal values and those of your company. This helps to continually infuse your staff with individuals who add to the cultural strength of your business rather than dilute it.

Next, reassess your relationships with vendors, partners, and customers. Every external interaction must be a reflection of your values. Aligning with businesses that share similar principles can create synergies and enhance trust. This alignment is particularly crucial in a 10X growth model; your partners become an extended part of your business, and dissonance in core values can result in conflict and inefficiency.

What about when things go awry? Upholding your values in the face of adversity is the ultimate litmus test. Let's say, unforeseen events threaten your operations – perhaps a downturn in the market or a supply chain breakdown. These are the moments where adherence to your values proves their worth. Staying true to them in tough times reinforces trust and loyalty among your team and customers. It sends a powerful statement about your reliability and long-term vision.

As you scale, it's tempting to let slide the small misalignments with core values for the sake of expedience. Beware of this trap! Little compromises lead to bigger ones, and before you know it, you've drifted off course. Regular check-ins on how well your business actions align with your core values are crucial. A yearly review or even a quarterly check-in can highlight areas where the business may be veering off track, allowing you to correct course before it's too late.

Integrating core values into your strategic planning also ensures that the goals you set reinforce what you stand for. When plotting your path to a 10X business value, choose strategies and tactics that abide by your core principles. Successful scaling is about growth that doesn't only look good on paper but also feels right at the core of your company's identity.

Let's not skirt around the fact that implementing core values requires consistent effort and sometimes hard decisions. There will be occasions when sticking to your values might mean passing up seemingly lucrative opportunities. However, in the long run, aligning with your values leads to sustainable growth and creates a business worth more not just in monetary terms, but also in reputational capital.

Finally, evolving your core values over time is natural as long as the evolution aligns with the overarching vision you hold. Your business doesn't exist in a vacuum—it grows and adapts. As it does, your values may also grow and adapt, provided they remain true to the fundamental ethos of your company. Nurturing an atmosphere of open dialogue about values encourages your team to embrace change while preserving the company's integrity.

Implementing core values isn't a one-off task—it's an ongoing mission. But the payoff transcends profit. It builds a business that stands tall with a clear identity and purpose, a business that people are proud to work for, and a business that customers trust and return to. That's the kind of business that not only commands a 10X valuation but also has the cultural fortitude to thrive beyond your exit. So let's embed those values deep. Let's live them out, loud and clear, in every aspect of our enterprise. This isn't just business; it's the legacy we're building, it's the mark we leave on the world. And it starts with what we value most.

Chapter 10: Outsourcing: Right-Sizing Your Labour Costs

It's time to talk strategy—tailoring your workforce without compromising your life's work. Imagine trimming down on excess expenditure without cutting corners on quality. Outsourcing stands as a masterstroke, allowing you to optimize your labor costs, tapping into a global talent pool that's agile, scalable, and cost-effective. But here's the kicker: it's not just about cutting costs; it's about strategic alignment, ensuring that every outsourced function and role fits snugly with your overarching goals. It's about creating that seamless extension of your operational family, one that carries the torch of your company's standards across international timelines. You'll navigate a maze of choices and decisions—what tasks to outsource, who to trust, and how to maintain control—to mold a team that's as lean as it is effective. There's merit in recognizing when to delegate, when to seek expertise, and when to free up your core team's bandwidth so their talents aren't just maintained but magnified. As you steer through this chapter, you'll unpack the trove of insights that allow you to reshape your labor costs, propelling you ever closer to that golden 10X exit. This isn't just cost-saving; it's business evolving.

The Role of Outsourcing in Business Efficiency

It's time to shine a spotlight on one of the most transformative strategies at your disposal – outsourcing. You've built a solid foundation, paved the way with digital prowess and streamlined operations, but let's propel your business into overdrive. Outsourcing isn't just a buzzword; it's a lever to catapult efficiency and prime your company for unfettered growth. Have you ever considered that the tasks eating up your precious time could be someone else's five-star service?

Think about the joy of peeling back layers of responsibility. You're not handing over the reins; you're lightening the load to focus on what matters – strategic growth and value multiplication. By outsourcing, you're tapping into a world brimming with talent eager to elevate your enterprise. They're specialists, obsessed with perfection in their niche, freeing you up to mastermind the broader strokes of your business canvas.

Cost effectiveness isn't just trimming expenses; it's smart investing. And there's no investment quite like outsourcing. It aligns cost with usage, ensuring you pay for productivity, not potential. Outsourcing converts fixed costs into variable ones, liberating your balance sheet and bestowing you with the agility of a gazelle in a field of slower, less innovative business models.

And you're not just looking for a quick fix. You're after longevity – a business poised to excel without you at the helm every moment. Outsourcing fosters this autonomy by embedding resilience and adaptability within your operation. Whether it's a call center, a production unit, or a shipping company, these external entities can turn scale into a non-issue, a minor detail effortlessly managed.

Risk – it's an inevitable part of business. Yet, who says you have to shoulder it alone? Outsourcing is a partnership, distributing the weight of risk across your network. When you outsource, you're sharing the responsibility for delivery and quality, mitigating any single point of failure. It is about expanding your safety net, ensuring continuity even when unforeseen events strike.

As we consider operational prowess, innovation often takes a back seat to day-to-day tasks. But with outsourcing, your business's creativity engine can rev at full throttle. Offload essential yet non-core activities and unleash a storm of innovation within your company. This lets you explore new horizons and create value-add propositions that can set you apart from the competition.

The connection between outsourcing and customer satisfaction is profound. Imagine delighting your customers with superior service levels without stretching your resources thin. Outsourcing firms often have the scale and expertise to provide services that meet or exceed customer expectations, ensuring you maintain a competitive edge.

Time – the most finite of resources, becomes abundant when you outsource. The hours saved by delegating tasks can be vectored towards strategic planning, networking, or simply recharging your own batteries to maintain the relentless pursuit of excellence. With outsourcing, you're not just buying services; you are purchasing time, the vital ingredient for a visionary leader like you.

Quality is non-negotiable, and outsourcing can elevate your standards to new heights. By partnering with best-in-class providers, you infuse your business with cutting-edge practices and quality benchmarks that can be hard to attain internally. This doesn't only boost your immediate product or service offering; it permeates your entire brand with a reputation for excellence.

Outsourcing can be your secret weapon for competition. Small companies turn into agile competitors, while large enterprises harness global talent to stay innovative and cost-effective. In a marketplace that's increasingly borderless, leveraging outsourcing is not just a tactical move; it's strategic warfare in the business arena.

In a world where adaptation determines survival and prosperity, outsourcing stands as a pillar of flexibility. Scale operations up or down without the pain and cost of hiring and layoffs. Outsourcing adapts to your business cycle, not the other way around, granting you the flexibility other businesses simply dream of.

While we've discussed the monumental perks of outsourcing, let's also acknowledge the managerial prowess it demands. It's not hands-off; it requires oversight, communication, and a solid framework for success. Like a skilled conductor leading an orchestra, you must harmonize the efforts of your outsourcing partners with that of your core team, crafting a symphony of business success.

Privacy and security – vital components of the modern business landscape, demand savvy handling, especially with outsourcing. Selecting partners that uphold the highest standards of data protection and confidentiality is paramount. This is not just about compliance; it's about safeguarding your customer trust and, ultimately, your reputation.

Now let's converge on the quintessence of a 10X business – the mindset that outsourcing is not an expense but an investment. An investment in focus, quality, growth, and in the freedom to build an empire that thrives with or without you at the desk. When it's time for you to take the bow, to make an exit that's both lucrative and tax-advantaged, you'll see the massive payoff from a well-orchestrated outsourcing strategy.

So, here you are, at the precipice of a bold decision. Will you clamp down on every operation, or will you pry open the doors to exponential efficiency through outsourcing? The next chapter unfolds when you decide to distribute the load, knitting a network of proficiency around your business, allowing you to soar to that 10X valuation. It's not just about growing a business; it's about growing a legacy.

Selecting the Right Tasks and Partners for Outsourcing is an art form in itself. It's about balancing the need for control with the freedom that comes from delegating. Imagine having a trusted partner take care of the tasks that, frankly, aren't the best use of your time. That's where outsourcing comes in, but it's not as simple as throwing tasks over the fence and hoping for the best.

First, let's get down to brass tacks. You need to identify the tasks you're looking to outsource. Think routine, time-consuming, and those that require specialized skills that don't align with your core competencies. There's a goldmine of tasks from customer service, bookkeeping, digital marketing, all the way to IT support that can be managed by someone else without missing a beat.

But here's the kicker: not all tasks are created equal. Picture this — you're eyeing to outsource your social media management. It's crucial, but it does not need your hands at the helm all the time. This task requires someone with the know-how to embody your brand's voice and engage with your audience authentically. A dash of creativity, a sprinkle of strategy, and a whole lot of consistency. That's what you're after.

Now, onto finding the partners. I'm talking about those game-changing collaborators who can take those tasks and elevate them. This isn't the Yellow Pages era; you're not flipping through a directory, picking out names at random. No, you're after partners who are proven, who understand your vision, and are as committed to your growth as you are. You want a partner, not a vendor. Someone who's invested in your success because, make no mistake, their success hinges on yours.

Quality is key. It might be tempting to go for the most wallet-friendly option, but take heed. A cut-rate service could end up costing you more in lost time, energy, and even customers. It's about finding that sweet spot where cost-effectiveness meets high-quality service. Think of it as an investment in your business's future.

And remember, communication is everything. You're looking for a partner whose communication is as clear as crystal. Misunderstandings can often lead to mistakes, and you don't have time for back-and-forths that end nowhere. A language barrier, time zone mismatch, or a simple lack of clarity can mean the difference between success and failure.

Let's chat about alignment. You want to outsource to those who get it, who get you. Culture fit matters because it aligns values, work ethic, and expectations. You're creating an extension of your team, and these individuals or firms must be on the same page. A misalignment here could be a thorn in your side, disrupting workflow and creating friction where you need smooth sailing.

And yes, it's crucial to check the reviews and references. A glossy website might catch your eye, but it's the experiences of others that will tell you if this partner walks the walk. Ring up their past clients, dig into their reputation, and find out if their service is all hat and no cattle. This due diligence might take time, but it's the fortress that protects your investment.

Don't forget to start small. You wouldn't propose marriage on the first date, would you? When you think you've found the right partner, trial a small project. This is your acid test, your no-commitment fling that can grow into a full-blown partnership. It allows you to see them in action without risking too much. Plus, it gives both parties the chance to assess the fit before signing the prenup.

Protect your intellectual property (IP) like it's the crown jewels. When you outsource, you're handing over bits of your business to outsiders. Make sure those non-disclosure agreements (NDAs) and IP contracts are airtight. It may seem like a chore, but it's the armor your business needs to avoid IP theft or leakage.

Set benchmarks and establish clear metrics for success. It's no secret – what gets measured gets managed. You need a clear, objective way to evaluate the performance of your outsourcing partner. Set up key performance indicators (KPIs) that align with your business objectives. Regular check-ins and reports keep everyone honest and moving toward the same end goal.

Finally, prepare for a change management strategy. Your in-house team needs to know that an outsourced partner is not a threat but an ally. Integrate them into your team with open communication and a clear explanation of how this partnership will elevate everyone's game. This ensures a smooth transition and avoids unnecessary resistance.

With all that said, don't lose sight of the human touch. Automation and systems are fantastic, but at the end of the day, people do business with people. Your outsourced partners should not only be proficient in their field but also human in their interactions. After all, it's the relationships and rapport that often make or break a business deal.

And when it all comes together, when you've selected the right tasks and the right partners, you'll see your business not just double or triple, but potentially 10X in value. Outsourcing, done right, is more than just a strategy; it's a force multiplier that propels you toward that tax-free exit — not as a whimper but as a battle cry of success.

Throughout this journey, hold onto the reins but let the horse run. Give your outsourcing partners enough autonomy to show their full potential yet maintain the oversight to ensure they are indeed pulling in the right direction. It's about trust but verify — fostering a partnership while protecting your vision.

To wrap it up, outsourcing isn't a checkbox to mark; it's a continuous quest for the perfect alignment of task, talent, and timing. As you push toward that 10X exit, keep in mind that the right outsourcing partners aren't just helping hands; they're co-strategists in your chess game of business. Choose wisely, nurture diligently, and watch as your empire expands, with the foundations laid for a grand and gratifying exit that's both triumphant and, importantly, tax-free.

Chapter 11: Tax-Free Selling: Preparing for the Exit

As we pivot from optimizing the sheer mechanics of business growth and operations, we find ourselves at the cusp of an exhilarating transition – the much-anticipated exit. It's not just about crossing the finish line; it's about leaping over it with finesse, and that's where tax-free selling enters like a hero in the eleventh hour. This is your guide to suiting up your business in the most attractive financial armour. Think of it as the ultimate life-hack for your wealth - where each decision you make now is a masterstroke in the grand chess game of financial planning. We're going to dive into how you can sculpt your business into the ideal candidate for a tax-advantaged sale. This isn't the everyday tax advice; this is the arsenal for the savvy business owner who knows that keeping more of your sale proceeds in your pocket is the smart play. You'll learn how to navigate this crucial phase, ensuring you emerge victorious and not ensnared in the all-too-common tax traps. Because let's be blunt - your legacy deserves to be measured in prosperity, not taxed into oblivion. Let's roll up those sleeves and prep your business for the grand exit that rewards your foresight with the financial freedom you've earned.

Structuring Your Business for a Tax-Advantaged Sale is often the jewel in the crown of a business owner's journey. Selling a business is not just about signing on the dotted line; it's about shaping your years of hard work into an entity that not just shines brightly in the buyer's eyes but also transfers to your bank account with minimal tax leakage. A savvy seller understands the intricacies of tax laws and uses them to their advantage. Let's dive into the nitty-gritty of selling your business in a tax-advantaged way.

First, it's essential to grasp that taxes can take a sizeable bite out of your sale proceeds. A business structured without tax planning might be subject to higher capital gains, state taxes, and possibly even trigger the dreaded alternative minimum tax. On the flip side, a well-structured entity aligned with a smart tax plan means more money in your pocket.

One critical step is choosing the right type of business entity. Whether you operate as an S Corporation, C Corporation, or LLC in the USA or a limited company or LLP in the UK, can have significant tax implications when it comes time to sell. More often than not, S Corporations and LLCs offer tax advantages because the gains are only taxed once at the shareholder level. C Corporations, on the other hand, can get hit twice— once at the corporate level and again at the shareholder level upon the disbursement of dividends, but currently, there are ways in which the business can be sold with no capital gains tax at all, and in the UK, the same applies, currently there are ways in which businesses can be sold very effectively and very quickly with minimal risk with no capital gains tax. Contact us for more details on this, both in the US and in the UK, and we'll update you with the latest, most advantageous ways to exit a business tax-free.

Years before the sale, consider the allocation of purchase price in anticipation of a future sale. Strategic allocation across different asset classes can result in differing tax treatments. For example, goodwill and other intangibles are taxed more favorably than tangible assets. Proper valuation and allocation can mean a substantial difference in tax liability.

Seller financing, often overlooked, can also provide tax breaks. Seller carry-backs can spread the tax burden over several years through instalment sales, potentially keeping you in a lower tax bracket than receiving a lump sum would.

In the case of strategic acquisitions made shortly before a sale, be conscious of the step-up in basis this can give to your assets. This step-up can reduce future capital gains taxes, often overlooked by those dazzled by the strategic play alone. Asset purchases, rather than stock purchases, can be instrumental in this regard.

Another strategy is the use of trusts. Charitable Remainder Trusts (CRTs) can allow you to defer capital gains taxes. At the same time, Grantor Retained Annuity Trusts (GRATs) can minimize estate taxes for your heirs, all while benefiting from the proceeds of the sale.

Business owners sometimes miss the opportunity to leverage life insurance in their tax strategy. Life insurance proceeds are typically tax-free in the USA and can be an efficient way to transfer wealth. Additionally, certain life insurance strategies can provide funds tax-free during your lifetime that can be used strategically as part of the sale process.

When considering any of these strategies, always involve your financial and legal advisors early. A coordinated approach is paramount as these professionals can help structure your business in compliance with current laws while aligning with your personal financial goals. We have a panel of both and can put you in contact if you'd like.

Audit your business activities and consult your advisors to identify any state-specific tax incentives or credits you may be eligible for. States can have vastly different laws that may allow you to minimize your tax footprint legally.

An often ignored but important piece of advice is to keep immaculate records. The more precisely and transparently your business's financial affairs are documented, the more ammunition you'll have to defend your tax positions. A lack of documentation is an open invitation for the IRS to question your reporting.

Before considering an outright sale, contemplate the option of a partial sale or a gradual transfer of ownership. This could involve selling a controlling interest while retaining a minority stake in the business, potentially bringing down your tax rates while still allowing you to partake in future growth.

If a family business is part of your legacy, consider an early transfer of ownership interests to family members through a Family Limited Partnership (FLP) or other family gifting strategies. Utilizing lifetime gift tax exclusions, you can potentially lower your taxable estate while setting the next generation up with a vested interest in the business.

Finally, keep a pulse on current and upcoming tax law changes. Tax codes are forever in flux, and staying informed ensures you're poised to adapt your strategy to maintain a tax-advantaged position. Watchfulness here can pay off enormously.

By aligning your business's structure and future sale with a tax-efficient strategy, you pave the way to retaining the utmost value from your efforts when that richly deserved sale materializes. You've not only built your business with dedication and savvy, but you'll also have the satisfaction of knowing you kept a lion's share of its value. Any business titan would agree – it's not just about making money, but also about keeping it.

Legal and Financial Planning for the Exit You've dedicated years, maybe even decades, to building your business into a towering achievement. Now, with the horizon of exiting gracefully and lucratively in sight, it's time to drill down into the legal and financial planning that will make for a smooth transition and an optimally beneficial sale. Let's lay the foundation brick by brick.

When we talk about legal and financial planning, we're spearheading straight into the heart of a strategic exit. This isn't just about getting your paperwork in order. It's a play of precision, timing, and keen awareness— a tightrope act where the safety net is woven from your legal foresight and financial acumen.

Start with a clear understanding of your business's legal structure. Whether it's an LLC, an S-corp, or another entity, each brings unique benefits and implications for an exit. Tweaking this structure pre-sale can optimize tax outcomes and appeal to informed buyers. Think of it as curating the most attractive package, not only in appearance but substance too.

Now let's talk about your dream team—attorneys, accountants, and financial planners who specialize in business exits. They're the maestros conducting the orchestra that will play the symphony of your successful exit. Embed them early in your exit strategy to ensure every move you make is in concert with your grand finale.

Don't overlook the emotional equity you've invested. You need to deal in clear-headed strategy, but it's important to acknowledge that there's a personal element to this transaction. A legal team aligns with your goals and understands this isn't just a business sale—it's a life transition. That kind of empathy paired with expertise is golden.

Contracts and agreements are your business's lifeblood. They should be pristine, comprehensive, and indisputable. This means revising and refreshing current agreements and ensuring every deal in place can withstand the scrutiny of due diligence. A missed clause or a lazy legacy contract can be a deal-breaker, or worse, a costly post-sale surprise.

Intellectual property represents a major value proposition in your sale. Secure all your trademarks, patents, copyright info—every piece of IP should be accounted for and protected. Buyers want security; they're buying your brand and its associated intellectual property. Make sure it's bulletproof.

Digs into the financial health of your business through meticulous analysis. Clean up your books and ensure your financial statements paint a clear picture. An unclear financial landscape is like fog on the path to exit —it causes uncertainty and doubt for potential buyers, two things that can diminish your business's perceived value.

Explore the timing of your exit. Timing can leverage market conditions, industry trends, and tax landscapes to net you a more lucrative payoff. It's not just about when you feel ready to sell; it's about when the market is ready to buy—at the right price.

Plan for debt management. If your business carries debt, develop a strategy for how it will be handled at the time of sale. Companies with clean balance sheets typically command higher prices. Work on paying down debt or ensure it can be smoothly transferred or settled as part of the sale.

Consider the role of earnouts and seller financing. These are tools that can be used to bridge valuation gaps and secure a higher purchase price, but they come with their own risks and rewards. Understanding the fine print of these financial arrangements is crucial to ensure they benefit you in the long run.

And don't forget the possibility of a partial exit. Perhaps you want to retain a stake in your business for personal reasons or to stay involved at a reduced level. This could provide ongoing income and a measure of control while still unlocking significant capital in the short term.

Plan for your capital gains. The tax implications of selling your business can be staggering. Strategic tax planning with professionals can help you navigate options like installment sales, trusts, and other financial structures that could mitigate the blow to your windfall.

Throughout this process, transparency with your management team and key employees is paramount. They can be vital allies in ensuring a seamless transition, so construct non-compete agreements, retention packages, and incentive plans that will preserve operational stability and keep the team motivated.

As you move toward the crescendo of this monumental period in your life, remember—it's more than just crossing Ts and dotting Is. It's about calibrating every aspect of your business with the fine-tuned intention of maximizing value, securing your legacy, and walking away with the freedom you've earned through your relentless pursuit of excellence. Let legal and financial planning be the launchpad of a brilliant finale to your entrepreneurial symphony, leaving the crowd—and your legacy, standing ovation-worthy.

Life After the Exit

After the climax of the sale comes the sweet release of culmination—Life After the Exit. This isn't just a restful hiatus; it's a vibrant, active stage of your journey where you chart new territories. Liberated from the day-to-day management, you're now primed to craft a life of vibrant experiences and impact. We get it, transitioning from the adrenaline-fueled marathon of entrepreneurship to the serene pace of post-exit life can be jarring. Remember, it's about relishing in the rewards that your hard work has earned. Imagine what you could do with that windfall sky-diving into your bank account—investing in dreams previously shelved, cultivating passions, or even fueling new ventures. The equity you've built in your business translates into a life redefined by choice, opportunities, and security. Embrace this transition as not an end, but an invigorating new beginning—your wealth isn't just in finances but in freedom, the true 10X multiplier.

Planning Your Post-Sale Life

The sun might be setting on your time helming your business, but let's spin this around - what a dawn it is for the rest of your life! Think about it. You've hustled, put in the elbow grease, and now stand at the precipice of a new chapter. As your thoughts shift from business strategies and growth metrics, they should now naturally migrate to the landscape of your post-sale life. This isn't a pause or a full stop; it's an exhilarating leap into a life that can be as structured or as freewheeling as you wish it to be.

Imagine waking to days that aren't structured around conference calls, investor meetings, or performance reviews. Instead, you're greeted with open-ended opportunities that align with passions and interests you've had on the backburner. Whether it's setting sail on the deep blue, immersing yourself in philanthropy, penning your memoir, or diving into a new business venture from the standpoint of experience – this is your time to shine in a whole new way.

Setting the stage for a rich and fulfilling post-sale life requires the same meticulous planning that you applied to growing your business. You'll want continuity for your financial security and activities that energize you. Craft a vision for your life that is bold and inspiring. Let this vision guide you, and don't hesitate to etch it in as much detail as you can fathom. In plotting out your future, consider not just the financial dimensions but also relationships, personal growth, recreation, and health.

Financial freedom is an obvious perk of selling your business, but money alone won't craft your new life's blueprint. Seize the moment to establish what makes you tick outside the business sphere. Got a hidden knack for painting or a burning desire to improve education in underprivileged areas? There are worlds to change and beauties to create – and you've got the ticket to be the catalyst.

Your post-sale life's foundation is anchored in your financial wellbeing. By now, you've hopefully structured the sale to be tax-efficient and maximized its proceeds. How you manage this monetary windfall will dictate the security and options available to you moving forward.

Investing thoughtfully is paramount. Diversify your portfolio, perhaps considering real estate, stocks, start-ups, or bonds. The key is to tailor your investment strategy to sustain and propel the lifestyle you envision.

Let's also address the wealth beyond the wallet - your time and health. Suddenly, you've got hours unfettered by the daily grind. Don't let them dissipate in front of a screen or evaporate in aimless activity. Cultivate new habits that fuel your energy - exercise, travel, learn a new language, or cook! As you shape your days, prioritize your well-being. After all, what good is financial security if you're not in shape to savor its fruits?

Social ties can often take a hit when you're at the helm of a successful business. Retirement, or semi-retirement, is your golden ticket to rekindle friendships and deepen family ties. It's also a chance to forge new connections with like-minded souls who share your newfound interests or passions. Surround yourself with positive influences that reflect and support your post-sale life's goals.

Charitable endeavors can offer a profound sense of purpose and fulfillment in your next chapter. Leveraging your skills, experience, and financial resources for a cause can extend the legacy of your business acumen beyond the sale. Decide what impact you'd like to leave on the world and chart a path towards it. Your capacity to build and grow a business is a testament to your potential to effect transformative change.

Mentorship can be a rewarding avenue to explore when you've sold your business. You possess a wellspring of knowledge that up-and-coming entrepreneurs both crave and desperately need. Unleash this treasure trove, shaping the future of the business world one protege at a time. It's a powerful vehicle for legacy-building and personal satisfaction.

And, of course, there's the potential for new business ventures. Many business owners discover that their entrepreneurial spirit doesn't retire even if they technically do. If a new project or startup beckons, take what you've learnt and let it escort you on this fresh journey. Embrace the fluidity between being an entrepreneur and an investor – for you, one chapter's end is just another's prologue.

Let's dive deeper into personal growth. You're not just a business owner; you're a multifaceted individual with unexplored depths. Now's the time to invest in yourself, take courses, read widely, and satiate that insatiable curiosity that's fueled your business journey. It's about enriching your inner world just as you've enriched your bank account.

You've got the resources now to design an environment that inspires and revitalizes you. Whether it's a beach house, an urban loft, or a country estate, your home can be your sanctuary and your launchpad. A space that reflects your achievements, tastes, and the life you're stepping into. Tailor it, love it, and let it be your rejuvenation hub.

Lastly, always remember to stay agile. Life is unpredictable, and even the best-laid plans may require tweaking. Stay open to new experiences, pursue interests, and be ready to adapt your plans as life unfolds. Just as in business, flexibility and resilience are your companions on this exhilarating ride.

Your post-sale life is a canvas, and you hold the brush. Whether it's peppered with audacious adventure, serene simplicity, or a fine balance of both, it's yours to paint. Take that lifetime of building, strategizing, and executing, and channel it into crafting a life of expansive horizons. Because, at the end of the day, life's too vast and bright to be confined to boardrooms and balance sheets, wouldn't you say?

Investing Your Windfall for Long-Term Security Now, as you flip the page from planning an exit to actually living it, your focus shifts from building wealth to preserving it. This journey, quite frankly, is about ensuring that the fruits of your labor sustain you, thrill you, and spill over to enrich the lives of those you care about. It's about making smart, calculated decisions—keeping your wealth growing and working as hard as you did to earn it.

You've worked tirelessly to scale your empire, and when the day comes to sign on the dotted line and sell, a delightful problem presents itself: you're suddenly flush with cash. While the temptation to splurge can be immense, remember, this windfall isn't just about you living the high life; it's the foundation of your financial legacy.

Forethought is your ally here. You're no stranger to calculated risk—after all, it's what got you here. Investing isn't about wheeling and dealing; it's about strategy, balance, and playing the long game. Having a structured investment plan in place is just as thrilling as any business venture you've undertaken, with the added bonus of long-term security for your golden years.

Think about diversification. Just like you wouldn't bet your company's future on a single client, don't bet your financial future on a single stock or asset. A mixed portfolio—stocks, bonds, real estate, maybe even some alternative investments like art or start-ups—spreads risk and increases the potential avenues for growth.

Get meticulous advice from winners in the financial world. They're the maestros who can orchestrate your investments to sing in harmony. A financial advisor's prowess can help you maneuver through market fluctuations and economic downturns, keeping you poised for growth without losing sleep over the regular ups and downs.

Let's cut to the chase: taxes. They're a bear, but a strategic investment approach can also mean smart tax planning. By positioning your investments in tax-advantaged accounts and considering the longevity of your investments, you can maximize your after-tax returns. It's like legal alchemy, turning potential tax burdens into golden opportunities for further wealth.

Think about your legacy, too. Estate planning goes hand in hand with investment. It's not just about what you leave behind, but also how you leave it. Be purposeful in setting up trusts, wills, and philanthropic endeavors which reflect what you stand for. This will ensure your wealth is a force for positive impact even when you're no longer at the helm.

Consider liquidity in your investment lineup. You'll want some assets you can easily convert into cash for unexpected expenses or seize new investment opportunities. Such fluidity ensures you're never caught in a tight spot or miss out on an advantageous play.

What about investing in yourself and your passions? Maybe there's an endeavor you've always wanted to explore, an education pursuit, or a hobby you wanted to turn into something more substantial. This investment creates a priceless sense of fulfillment and often opens doors to unexpected financial growth.

Don't overlook the power of passive income streams. Investments that keep putting money in your pocket without daily effort can be a game-changer. Real estate rentals, dividend-yielding stocks, or even writing a book about your business success can establish legacy income. The beauty here is in creating a consistent cash flow that doesn't demand your constant attention.

Now, let's talk impact investing. People and the planet matter, and as a seasoned business owner, you know that socially responsible investing isn't just good karma; it's good business. Funds with a focus on ethical practices often perform as well—or better—than their less-conscious counterparts. It's your chance to make money and make a difference.

Also, know when to adapt. Markets evolve, opportunities shift, and your financial plan should be agile enough to pivot with the times. Have regular check-ins with your advisors to assess your portfolio's performance and adjust as needed to stay aligned with your goals and the economic landscape.

Through it all, keep your eye on the prize: long-term security. It's not just about making your money last; it's about leveraging it into a dynamic, yet sturdy safeguard for your future. A fortress of financial stability if you will, built from the bricks of smart, diverse investments, fortified by sage advice and tax efficiency.

Most importantly, remember: you've earned this. Every late night, every tough decision, every risk that paid off—it's culminated in this moment. Respect the effort that it took by treating this windfall with the same care and strategic brilliance you applied to your business. This is how you ensure that its benefits will continue to amply flow, not just for you but for generations to come.

In the end, planting seeds for long-term security isn't just a financial decision; it's creating peace of mind. It's knowing you're leaving a legacy that's not just wealthy, but also wise, abundant, and reflective of the life you've lived and the values you hold dear. So let's forge ahead with confidence. Your future, after all, is waiting to be built on the smart decisions you make today.

Your 10X Journey

You've traversed the exhilarating path of scaling your business with the vision of a 10X exit. Each chapter you've explored is a building block, an essential step towards the transformation of not just your business, but your life. This isn't the end but the beginning of something new—your 10X journey. As we wrap up this roadmap, it's crucial to recall that the principles and strategies shared are not one-off tasks, but components of a continual cycle of growth, refinement, and innovation.

Your ambition for explosive growth is not only admirable, but wholly attainable. The energy you've invested in envisioning your 10X future provides the clarity needed to be decisive in your actions. Remember, the pathway to enlarging your business tenfold is anchored in the clear vision you've crafted. This vision will guide you like a lighthouse when the waters of business become tumultuous and the decisions seem overwhelming.

Embracing digital marketing was a game changer, wasn't it? The online world, with its multitude of platforms and strategies, can no longer be an afterthought for businesses that aspire to grow exponentially. You've learned to harness the power of Facebook and Google ads, integrating online sales funnels that are not just functional but formidable. This isn't the end of the campaign trail but a segment that requires you to evolve constantly with the digital landscape.

Mastering social media is akin to mastering the art of conversation in a crowded room. Your strategies for success on platforms like YouTube, Facebook, Instagram, and TikTok open up a world where your brand narrative can flourish. The viral nature of these platforms can catapult your presence to new highs. The important lesson here is to keep the conversation going, growing, and gleaming with authenticity.

When it comes to scaling with acquisitions, recall the transformative potential of doubling your business size. Navigating acquisitions is much like navigating the high seas—for safe passage, one must be well-versed with the maps and compasses of due diligence and strategic fit. Remember, while the acquisition itself can happen in an afternoon, integration is where the true skilfulness is demonstrated.

Face-to-face sales have been a high-impact tool for businesses for decades. By leveraging your contacts and building personal rapport, you've seen how it's possible to close deals and scale revenue. Practising these skills, maintaining relationships, and furthering personal connections will continue to be a cornerstone of your success.

Operations and efficiency go hand-in-hand. You've seen the importance of a smooth-running operation and the role of technology in enhancing workflows. These aren't items to check off a list, but continuous endeavours. Always seek newer, better technologies and methods to streamline your operations, and never settle for the status quo.

System and processes are indeed the backbone of scaling, and they demand ongoing attention. The development and optimization of your business systems should be an exercise in constant improvement, aligning with your scaling aspirations. As your business grows, your systems must grow with it, both in complexity and robustness.

Let's talk leadership—identifying, cultivating, and retaining top talent. The management team you've built won't just sustain your growth; they'll be the force multiplier for it. Invest in your people, and empower them to make decisions that align with the vision. Remember that empowerment leads to autonomy, and autonomy leads to success.

It can't be overstated—company culture is pivotal. The 10X growth you seek thrives in a culture centred on core values. These aren't mere words, but the ethos that every team member embodies. Sustain and nurture this culture, for it makes your business not only a place of work but a place of passion and purpose.

Outsourcing has shown you the power of right-sizing your labour costs. It's important to note, however, that as your business evolves, so too will your outsourcing needs. Always be on the lookout for tasks and roles that can be efficiently managed through partners, allowing your core team to focus on critical growth activities.

And as for preparing for the tax-free selling—it's the capstone of your financial prudence. By structuring your business with an eye towards a tax-advantaged sale, you are setting the stage for a rewarding exit. This is not just an exit strategy but a masterclass in legacy building.

The exit is not the final act; it paves the way for 'life after the exit.' Strategy doesn't end once the sale is complete. Post-sale life planning and investing your windfall wisely will ensure that the value you've created extends beyond the confines of your business and secures your long-term security.

As you stand at this juncture, looking back at the journey and forward towards the horizon, remember that everything you've learned, accomplished, and aspired to be is a testament to your resilience, innovation, and drive. You are not just a business owner; you are a visionary on a never-ending quest to build, scale, and transcend limits.

Your 10X journey doesn't conclude with the final page of this book. It continues every day, with every decision and action you take. Embrace the lessons, live the strategies, and embody the spirit of growth. Keep your sights set on that glorious horizon, and let your business—and your life—reflect the magnificence of your dreams.

Appendix A: Resources for 10X Growth and Tax-Free Exits

You've navigated the ins and outs of scaling your business, learned the art of digital marketing, and mastered the essentials of a winning culture. Now it's time to consolidate your gains and chart the course for a tax-efficient, prosperous exit. In this appendix, we're honing in on high-octane resources that will fuel your journey to that 10X growth and seamless, tax-exempt exit you've envisioned.

It's a complex climb, but the view from the peak is worth every step. Consider this appendix your personal sherpa, guiding you through the final ascent. Let's dive into the resources that can make your business soar and your exit strategy as smooth as silk.

Educational Resources and Guidance

- **Blogs and Journals**: Start with a regular diet of insights from top business journals. Frequent places like the Harvard Business Review, Forbes, and Entrepreneur for groundbreaking ideas and trends in business growth and exiting strategies.
- **Books**: Stack your shelves with game-changing reads that cover growth strategies and tax planning. Titles by renowned strategists and financial experts will act as a beacon, illuminating your path to a tax-efficient exit.
- **Podcasts**: Audio content is ripe with knowledge. Subscribe to podcasts that feature interviews with business leaders who've successfully grown and exited their companies. They're a goldmine of actionable advice.

Online Courses and Workshops

Invest time in online courses and workshops. High-caliber institutions often offer programs focused on business growth, management, and even specific tax planning techniques. Keep learning; it's a lever for leverage.

Professional Associations and Networking Groups

- **Industry-specific associations**: These can give you insights specific to your sector, especially on how to manage growth and prepare for an eventual sale.
- **Entrepreneurial groups**: Networks like EO (Entrepreneurs' Organization) and YPO (Young Presidents' Organization) are fertile grounds for sharing knowledge and learning from those who have scaled the summit before you.

Financial and Tax Advisors

Building a relationship with seasoned financial and tax advisors can't be overstated. These professionals will be imperative in structuring your business for a tax-advantaged exit.

Legal Expertise

Connect with a legal team well-versed in corporate sales and acquisitions. They'll help safeguard your interests and ensure that your exit is not only profitable but fully compliant with tax legislation.

Business Valuation Services

Understanding the worth of your business is crucial. Employ business valuation experts to accurately gauge your company's market value—it's pivotal in negotiating a deal that truly reflects your business's worth.

With these resources at your fingertips, you're poised to push beyond the boundaries of business as usual. As you wrap your mind around the wealth of information and support available, let yourself be invigorated by the potential that lies ahead. It's not just about growth; it's about monumental, stratospheric success accompanied by a graceful and smart exit.

Grasp these tools, hone your knowledge, network vigorously, and embrace the expertise of advisors. You're not just running a business; you're crafting a legacy that can prosper beyond your leadership and provide you with a well-deserved, tax-astute reward for your years of dedication.

Let's move beyond mere success into the realm of legend. Your empire awaits, and the map to your treasure lies within the pages you've just absorbed and the resources outlined herein. Forge ahead, the summit is in sight, and the horizon is yours for the taking.

Appendix B: Checklists and Templates for Implementation

When the time comes to turn visions into reality, roll up your sleeves and brace yourself for the transformative journey ahead. You're not just building a business; you're architecting a legacy. To aid in this noble endeavor, we've distilled the essence of strategy down to practical checklists and templates. These tools are your roadmap to amplifying business value and achieving a seamless, tax-advantaged exit.

Business Vision Checklist

Start with a clear vision. Where is it you're going? How will you know you've arrived? This checklist will help you define your goals, sharpening the focus on your destination.

- Clarify your long-term business goal.
- Establish measurable targets for growth and value.
- Determine your desired exit timeline.
- Identify potential roadblocks and opportunities.

Value Assessment Template

To magnify your company's worth, you first need to understand its current value. This template will guide you through assessing the financials and unique selling propositions that define your business's market position.

1. Financial performance overview
2. Competitive advantage breakdown
3. Key metrics tracker for ongoing evaluation

Digital Marketing Plan

Digital marketing can be a goldmine with the right strategy. Use this plan to carve your path through SEO, social media, and online advertising—ensuring every click brings you closer to the 10X goal.

- Objectives and key results for digital marketing initiatives
- Content calendar for social media channels
- Budget and ROI tracker for online campaigns

Acquisition Strategy Template

Grow your empire through smart acquisitions. This template will help you identify targets, conduct due diligence, and integrate new assets as you swiftly double your business size.

1. Identifying potential acquisition targets
2. Diligence checklist
3. Post-acquisition integration plan

Sales Optimization Checklist

Maximize revenue with every handshake. This checklist will reinforce your face-to-face sales strategy, ensuring you're leveraging relationships and closing deals like a seasoned pro.

- Key principles of rapport and trust-building
- Scripts and techniques for effective negotiation
- Tracking and improvement system for sales conversions

Operational Efficiency Template

Streamlining operations is non-negotiable for exponential growth. Use this template to refine your processes, elevating your business performance to unprecedented heights.

1. Process mapping for key business operations
2. Efficiency audit to identify bottlenecks
3. Technology implementation plan

Management and Team Template

Finding and nurturing the right leaders is critical. This templated approach to team management will help you build a self-sustaining management team, primed for success.

- Leadership role and responsibility outlines
- Training and development programs
- Performance evaluation and feedback systems

Company Culture Development Plan

Culture is the heartbeat of your business. Craft and reinforce a 10X culture with a detailed plan that permeates every level of your organization, encouraging alignment with core values and driving exponential growth.

- Core values and company mission statement
- Staff engagement and retention strategies
- Cultural initiatives and community building activities

Exit Strategy Checklist

Exiting tax-free is an art—one that requires meticulous planning and strategic structuring. This checklist will ensure you're equipped for a graceful, profitable exit from the business you've so passionately built.

- Tax considerations and financial structuring before the sale
- Succession planning for a smooth transition
- Post-sale financial planning to secure your future

Every item on these lists, every section of the templates, brings you closer to your 10X dream—10X the value, 10X the impact, 10X the legacy. This isn't just about growth; it's about transformation. It's about creating something of such value that when the time comes to pass the torch, you do so not just with financial security, but with the profound satisfaction of having scaled the mountain and planted your flag firmly at the summit.

Printed in Great Britain
by Amazon

44534881R00066